Life is a Dream

A Journey of a Cancer Survivor

William Bulla

authorHOUSE

AuthorHouse™
1663 Liberty Drive
Bloomington, IN 47403
www.authorhouse.com
Phone: 833-262-8899

Published by AuthorHouse   05/21/2021

ISBN: 978-1-5246-2296-1 (sc)
ISBN: 978-1-5246-2297-8 (hc)
ISBN: 978-1-5246-2295-4 (e)

Library of Congress Control Number: 2016912586

Print information available on the last page.

About the Editor

René Luptak was born in 1961 in Brooklyn NY. She moved to Florida during elementary school and graduated from Pine View School for the Gifted in Sarasota Florida in 1979. She attended Emory University in Atlanta, GA and graduated with a BBA in Accounting in 1983.

René currently lives in Boca Raton and is a Principal and Recruitment Manager for Bartlett & Associates, a healthcare recruiting firm that specializes in partnering with companies in the skilled nursing/long-term care industry.

René and William first met at the Boca Raton Tennis Center in 2008. Several years later, they ran back into each other while William was completing his book about his journey as a leukemia survivor. Moved by his heartfelt objective, René assisted William in the revision of his book. The collaboration has been a journey in itself, and the friendship and respect for each other that has developed is never-ending.

Author's Intro

Our lives are always touched by major or lesser events that can change our course of destiny instantly, either in a positive or negative way. However, it is human nature to have a tendency to assume that in this complex world of ours every single day seems to rotate in a positive direction. Not so is the real case, because we must realize that fate sets the pace for all these intricacies, obviously, being a major contributor to life's evolution stage. Great Scots! Suddenly, just like fingers snapping, the world can turn around in a certain fashion. In a matter of seconds, intense and drastic changes can occur, affecting what is all around us in our daily routine life because of a positive and satisfying, or unpleasant, turn of events. Obviously, it can be general news, a disclosure of success, or a tragic personal event, affecting the course of action for that matter. None of us living mortals can be spared from such psychological, or physical, imposing complexity of life's mission.

Preface

Today, January 11, 2010, shall mark the date I am embarking on a voyage to share personal experiences that will cover some of the most extraordinary passages registered in the annals of my life. It will be a goal to achieve beyond any unpredictable expectations. There will be several chapters, involving stages very condensed, illustrating my background and place of origin and the first stage of my life from crawling to 20 years of age.

It will be followed by a second stage involving some of the most detailed experiences that any human could really endure while battling one of the most devastating illnesses during a long period of time. To be almost exactly described as absolutely a miracle from above, destiny had it that I had a mission on earth.

The third stage will illustrate how some of my goals were accomplished, after being out of remission and the aftermath. The fourth and final stage will be a period of incertitude deceptions and what I personally consider a critical part of my existence, years of endless struggling for survival, and keeping my personal statute intact over all tragedy.

This book is dedicated with my profound love to some terrific persons who have played a tremendous role in my life. They have been the spiritual and corporal inspiration, the fountain of knowledge solemnly bestowed on my soul quite indeed...to say the least.

My beloved mother Ana Gonzalez, whose wisdom, humbleness, and profound faith inspired me to follow exactly her disposition for the years to come. She was my entire life inspiration, the reason why I became later on what I am.

My dear brother Roberto, whose endless work came to my rescue when I needed someone the most. My former wife Clemencia, whose confidence, trustworthiness and unimaginable personal support, contributed to my recovery, perhaps during the most critical period of my life.

My adorable daughter Ingrid, whose tender age was witness to my battle against Leukemia (blood cancer). And two wonderful friends, Lawrence Chaleff and Joan Morsan, who unquestionably have displayed such an unselfish loyalty in good and perilous times over 40 years.

Also those who have come to my spiritual rescue on so many occasions, wonderful souls that I shall carry in my thoughts until the end of time. God bless them all collectively because without their unselfish support, a well done task, I probably might have succumbed earlier in my existence. There is not a single day in my life that I might have forgotten them in my daily prayers or solitude, not at all!

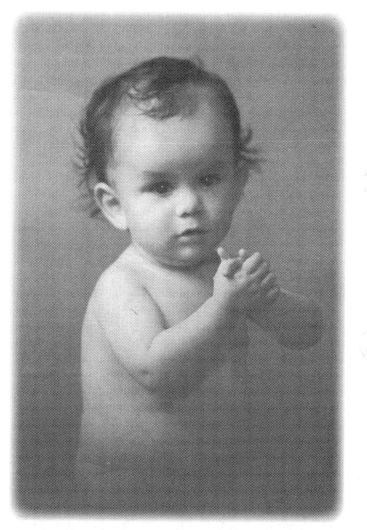

1943, during my "tender infantile stage", 1 year old

1955, 13 years old

November 15, 1963
Birthday celebration with Clementia at the Jack
Dempsey Restaurant months after diagnosis

1968, 4 years after diagnosis

Passport Photo

1988, Ingrid William Clemencia

1972, Robert in New York City

1949, from top left, Marco Edward, Mother,
William Herman, Joseph Robert

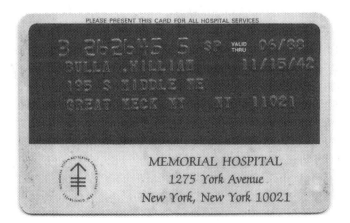

Chapter 1

My life began during one of the bloodiest global war conflict eras in mankind's history, the Second World War. According to historians, it has been described as an Apocalypse in human annals. Therefore, I describe myself as a product son of the Second World War. Even though I was too young to be aware of whatever was taking place, I have reached the conclusion I am one of the luckiest persons alive since time of my conception. In chapters ahead, it will be clearly explained in detail the reasons for producing such a statement.

For personal records, my place of birth was Santa Fe de Bogota, capital city of Colombia, South America, and my day of birth: November 15, 1942. Bogota is a lovely city located on an immense valley 2,609 meters in altitude above sea level. It is surrounded by some of the most spectacular mountain chain scenery found anywhere on Earth with a delicate spring-like climate with temperatures soaring an average of 16 degrees Centigrade or 60 degrees Fahrenheit.

The first four years of my life were virtually spent in obscurity, the reason why I have not a single recollection, whatsoever, as to what transpired either in historical or contemporary events. By the time I was over four years of age, I finally reached the zenith of my tender infantile stage, no longer living in limbo. I began to remember major events and the rest was just a typical part of human development.

There were three specific recollections that I have from when I was just over 4 years of age. The earliest one was when I was standing on the second floor corridor overlooking the patio below, and watching my father seated in a strange position inside of a little room with the door half way open. Later I found out it was where waste was discharged, better known as the rest room.

The second important experience as far as I am concerned, took place at the time when my dear mother's neighbors, the Aguilera family, extended an invitation to us to spend a week away at their state farm about two hours from home. It was really stunning to me to be in a farm surrounded by a unique scenario of animals all around and my brother taking me for a short ride together sitting in the horse saddle. What a spectacle it was watching how the cows were milked, producing such a splendorous pearl like fluid.

Later on that week, I heard for the first time a tragedy that occurred at the farm when a cat fell into a submerged tank container used specially to hold the natural sugar cane juice and boiled to process the product. I do recollect the confusion and indecision ensued next by some workers trying to recover the poor cat's body, but all was in vain. I guess when thinking back about the incident, that the poor creature was melted by the intense boiling thick liquid, that accident turned out to be my first exposure to tragedy for the rest of my life.

Finally, the third memory was when I reached my fifth year of life; I recall being registered in school for kindergarten. I was extremely lucky because my Godmother was the director and owner of the educational institution where I was registered. This gave me a sense of security for my first day of school.

Going back to the earliest 1950's year, in my tender life somewhere close to 7 years of age, I became obsessed when for the first time I saw a beautiful tennis court. I could not stop from dreaming; I had a profound desire to learn how to play the game with which my parents could not support me financially. I was told it was a very expensive sport, exclusively for the very wealthy and high society families. Therefore, my dreams of playing this fascinating game came to a long halt. Even in my childish mentality I was able to comprehend my parents' financial position.

However, it never stopped me from walking a long distance, maybe about an hour and a half to the National Park in Bogota City, to see some of the very distinguished players enjoying this fascinating recreational game, and watching ladies and gentlemen of elegant society as well. In those days, I came to see probably the best player that Colombia has ever produced. His name was William Alvarez from the city of Medellin,

State of Antioquia, very slender, tall and handsome and whose major accomplishment was reaching the quarter finals at the prestigious British Wimbledon Open, somewhere around the year 1956. He played an exhibition game against a well-known, high society player by the name of Dario Behard whose background was German descent. It was such a memorable spectacle; it really created an impact for the rest of my life. Little did I know while still living in Bogota, that decades later, I would be watching my adorable daughter Ingrid escalating to the College ranking level and setting records. During those years, whenever she played and competed, she exceeded all my expectations.

The only time that I was fortunate to own a tennis racket, happened on one occasion when my cousin Dario Duarte, who was working for the National Army in the Account Department, gave me as a gift an old tennis racket, which I was immensely grateful for indeed. What a thrill! I felt rewarded having my own tennis racket. It became my favorite toy until the day came when my parents sent me overseas to live with my brother Robert in the city of New York, USA.

I had a horrifying personal experience in those days when I was 9 years old. It happened one early afternoon when my mother and some relatives came back from the cemetery bringing a medium size wood box. Years later, it was described to me as an urn where ashes from the deceased member remain deposited for a final rest, at any particular choice location. In the meantime, according to traditions, for the time of three days a table covered with a mantle and some lighted candles next to the urn would serve as an altar, for homage and praying at home.

I was so extremely curious to see what was inside of it that I went upstairs alone to the second floor, and walked into the room where the urn was laid. Since I was not tall enough at this time, I proceeded by moving a chair and going on top of the mantel for a better view. Great Scott, as soon as I took a glimpse at the inside content, I panicked, jumped from the chair, and ran downstairs screaming. Throwing myself into my mother's arms I exclaimed loudly to her that I did not want to die, therefore, I wanted to become a doctor so I would never die! You see, at that tender age I was under the impression that doctors were immortals, per se.

The years went by and before I knew it my adolescent years made their triumphant entrance unto my body creating sort of the most unbelievable discoveries, both physical and psychological of which I had never previously been aware, perhaps because of the lack of communication with my parents. Well, on second thought, years later, I came to realize that any questions or doubts in evolutionary development would be some kind of taboo and would only be discovered through other sources of knowledge like infiltrating confidential friends, or through book illustrations. It used to be, at that time, the most appropriate approach to gaining a good solid, well founded acknowledgment.

Continuing with my adolescent exposure to facts of life and new experiences that I came across those early years, during the year 1956, my dear mother extended the most sincere hospitality to one her nephews Dario Duarte, his lovely wife Lucila Zambrano, and their two children. They stayed for a period of four months by the time residential visas had been issued with destination to the United States of America. During the time spent in mother's home, Lucila and I began to develop some sort of mutual tender feelings, and there were occasions when we grew fonder of each other. In an innocent fashion, my inert feelings turned quite volcanic, because of my immaturity, never mentioning to her what was happening and personally concerning my inner emotions. Later on as I woke up into a reality stage and I developed a platonic-like love towards her, she really became my obsession, the woman of my dreams, the epitome of perfection and beauty.

On one particular occasion she asked my mother for permission to take me to the cinema and my mother allowed me to do so. She took me by my hand and walked out directly towards the theater to enjoy the premier movie featured. I was so excited, I had delirious feelings; while watching whatever was going on the screen, I was in a state of fascination contemplating her profile. What a night! Some magical experience that would be remembered for the rest of my life, also because she was very much kind, and similarly responsive to me in a very special way.

Finally the day arrived for us to say good bye and Lucila, Dario, and the children departed for that long journey to what would be their new adopted country, the United States of America. Ever since then, I never heard from her again. The years passed by, she was in the most profound part of my heart. Whenever I had any opportunity, my dear mother would be the intermediate person to whom I would be questioning Lucila's whereabouts, but all in vain. My mother had vaguely any information until one day she received the news that they had returned to Colombia, reason unknown. Upon their return, I already had moved to the United States some years earlier, and my entire family had settled permanently in this wonderful country that we adopted with grace.

How could I forget the first young lady who in my recollections became my first sweetheart? I met her almost at the time when the wake up experience that I had with my beloved Lucila was taking place. More than half a century has gone by, yet her name I still remember as if it was only yesterday. A pretty girl with a cinnamon-like skin complexity and extremely attractive dimples, my unforgettable Nancy Restrepo Diaz, who was about the same age as me. Sometimes my heart wonders how she may be doing, and what a thrill it would be to see her again and hold her very tenderly in my arms. Of course, that would be the case if she still is alive; I honestly hope so.

Throughout my school years, numerous memorable events took place, and as I was growing physically and becoming a young adult and psychologically gaining unlimited wisdom at gigantic steps, my life was taking a complete turnaround. I felt power in my hands, invincible, just like a formidable warrior. I had reached the conclusion in my naive state of mind that the world was to be at my disposal, a real utopia.

As the time went by, I became very fond and much involved with anything that has to do with sports; delirium was the order of the day! I started to show some talent to my superiors. Finally, upon personal decision, I took self-initiative and the rest became history, when on a particular occasion, I attended a Football League try-out in my neighborhood. Soon after, I was recruited to a local team by the name of Col Carmen, under the direction of an excellent school teacher with impressive athletic credentials. Our first season tournament turned out to be a rewarding experience. Our team finished with an acceptable record, nothing to be ashamed of at all; we came to appreciate the fruits of our effort and commitment. Shortly after there was another consolation tournament in which we went all the way to the finals with an impressive statistical result. We went as far as to play the championship final at the National University Stadium Alfonso Lopez. Needless to mention, it turned out to be a terrific feeling of self-esteem playing in front of hundreds of spectators. A date to remember for the rest of my life was winning my first trophy medal; it became the foundation of my athletic achievements in future years to come.

On one occasion, in 1956, the family was affected severely, especially my beloved mother, upon receiving sad news from grandmother and close relatives who lived nearby at the town of Mosquera, where my mother's family had resided and still do at present time. My beloved grandfather Papa Punito, the very dear way he used to be called by every member of the family without any exceptions, had passed away after a heart seizure at the age of 86. As far as I do remember in the last couple of years prior to his death, his body was starting to degenerate, weakened characteristics of old age syndrome. Wake arrangements were done according to old traditional practice. There was a celebration in the house living room where a temporary table setting was covered with flowers, candelabras, and the statue of our lord. The casket was resting with the top open and exposed for viewing, his immobile body embalmed and laying in a white silk-like sheet which gave the impression he was just only sleeping.

The funeral day religious service took place at the imposing Mosquera Catholic Church, which gathered a tremendous participation from family, relatives, close friends, public and private representatives, local Government and the business sector, since he was so popular. He was well known in the surrounding communities because of his tireless unselfish caring dedication, not only to the welfare of his family but to hundreds of citizens who worked under his belt, and also for his philanthropic contributions for those who were dispossessed. Perhaps one of his major contributions was the donation of one of his properties to the Salesian Religious Organization for a construction project, a new University erected within the Town Center. Coincidentally, my late father became part of the Salesian Alumni and graduated with high honors with a Doctorate Degree in Agronomy during the early 1930s. Unfortunately, more than a half century has passed, and yet no recognition has been rendered by an historical account honoring my grandfather's philanthropic life missionary work.

Right after the funeral ceremony was officially concluded, we all proceeded to take the body to the already allocated Family Mausoleum, located outside of the town limits approximately half a mile away. The casket was carried by his sons and grandchildren on their shoulders. While following the caravan, I was so touched by the painful event. I was affected by all the pre and post family feuds and reminiscing about my Grandfather's determination to sacrifice many of his dreams in order to care for his family; they inspired me to become what I am today and changed the course of my life. Damascus strikes again! He worked so much that he hardly ever traveled, only a couple of times to the Northern Colombia region, according to my Mothers' version. At that precise moment, I made a major decision that would have an impact on the rest of my life. I promised to the Almighty, after deep soul searching, that I would direct my destiny into a style of simple honest living renouncing all pompous standards. I would carry out a mission to completely dedicate my life to serve my brethren dutifully in an unselfishness manner. Grandfather's tombstone, his final perpetual resting place, became for me the beginning of a new era.

There has never been any sorrow for taking on such a profound commitment, on the contrary, immense personal pride.

For the four years after my Grandfather passed away, every day went by without any major events. Life was simple and I was turning wiser and very much involved in different type of activities and growing diligently. Upon my mothers' personal encouragement, I started to take piano lessons under the tutelage of an accomplished music teacher by the name of Olga Saenz, an excellent lady with some remarkable character qualities. I really enjoyed learning how to master the complex instrument. By the time I already had studied the technical basics, within a short time of maybe 4 months or so, I was able to play some non-complex simple classical music arrangements.

Chapter 2

About six months before the year 1958 ended, I was informed by my parents of the great news that I would be traveling away to the United States of America to live with my older brother Robert. He already had been a permanent resident in the city of New York since the year 1957. I was very much excited indeed, however, there were some mixed feelings. Leaving my parents, the rest of my family, and many of my childhood dear friends and acquaintances, would not be so easy for me to accept. Leaving all of the good memories behind was a major concern to me, and why not? They did represent the years dating back to my entire childhood and what followed into my adolescent stage.

Little did I realize during the Christmas and New Year holiday celebrations, that it would mark the last time I would be spending them in Colombia, reunited with those who were so dear to me. I had emotional introverted feelings to be remembered for the rest of my mortal life. I really did not shed any tears during this time but it would strike my soul. Later on while being so far away from home, the solitude, the uncertain state of mind, almost became victorious once I had reached my final destination.

Suddenly, the long awaited day for departure arrived so fast, like a meteoroid traveling throughout the Universe with limitless immensity. It was somewhere about 7:00 A.M. when my beloved Mother came to my room to wake me up. She approached my bed, immediately kissed me for the last time, expressing some sort of uneasy feelings. However, I was extremely happy, aware I was going to a distant land where a bright future would probably be in store for me. I took a shower and dressed with a nice suit, properly attired for the long planned trip traveling into an unknown destiny. I also had my traditional breakfast consisting of "Changua" a typical traditional light soup, a fruit parlay chocolate cup, a slice of bread and butter, and oatmeal cereal to complement my palate and physically prepare for the long journey soon to start.

Once I had finished my breakfast, my mother left the luggage by the corridor and directed me to the patio where my brothers Marco and Herman, sister Maria Amparo, and domestic household servants gathered to wish me a safe trip. It was such an atmosphere surrounded with quite emotional feelings. It would mark perhaps the last time seeing these wonderful domestic workers.

Before I realized it, a taxi cab driver arrived just on time to pick up my parents and me. Everything happened so quickly while being sort of distracted overlooking some of the places very familiar to me, where I had spent great times. We went directly cross-town to the outskirts of the City of Bogota to Techo International Airport. Once there, we were instructed by officials to provide all of the required appropriate documentation at the Customs Service Center. During the waiting period prior to departure, my mother took me to the side somewhere and started to prepare me, finally, for what I consider my first experience as a separation from her never before done, going far away to live with my brother Robert. A couple of hours elapsed and all of us passengers were requested to carry the proper identification in hand and to proceed towards the exterior where a plane was going to take us beyond. Naturally, I took a few minutes to kiss my father and mother with some emotional feelings and tears in our eyes to say the least. Alas! The moment of truth had finally arrived and the pilgrimage started in a straight direction to the airport, my heart pumping faster and faster. I am feeling as if my lower torso is definitely ready to succumb to the nervous system, no other explanation, in anticipation for whatever is lying beyond.

That morning the sky was so clear, the perfect atmospheric conditions existed for the plane to take off. Once I came to the mobile stair, I started to walk up into the plane. Before going to my designated seat, I took a last glimpse, waving to my parents with vigorous agitation. I was in state of shock, to say the least. Well, never before in my life did I have the experience of traveling by airplane. It was first time indeed, wow! Apparently good luck was with me, no doubt, to my surprise the passenger seated next to me turned out to be an attractive lady who was traveling back to New York where she was a resident for quite a number of years. She had graduated from a prestigious University in the borough of Manhattan, N.Y. City.

Once seated, prior to beginning our move onto the runway, I could not help but notice that the plane interior was slightly on a declined position. The decor and room space were very comfortable. There was a good lighting system and 2 seat rows on one side and 2 seat rows on the opposite side separated by the alley in the middle with small windows just large enough to have a perfect view. Finally, the Captain, the co-pilot, and the Flight Engineer made an announcement that the airplane was ready for takeoff. In the meantime, the Stewardesses are requesting that everyone accommodate the safety belts and seatbacks properly. Before you know it, all of a sudden, some strange sounds start developing. I am seriously becoming a little bit nervous. It is my first flying experience, therefore, what do I know anyway? At this instance my dear companion advices me to remain calm; there is nothing to fear whatsoever according to her statement. In one, two, three, I am overlooking the city from the skies, feeling so much emotion it is hard to believe. Some of the clouds already are starting to embrace the airplane and it is completely covered, creating poor visibility all around. Shortly after, I am seeing the city disappear far beyond the distant horizon, a very interesting scenario just like a magic touch. The City of Santa Fe De Bogota that had witnessed me being born a long time ago, now was far out of reach to the naked eye.

Once the airplane has reached the desired altitude, the pilots are announcing over the electronic system that in a few minutes we shall be flying over the majestic "Los Andes mountain chains, which connect an incredible extension starting at the extreme end of Patagonia and dividing two countries, Argentina and Chile at America's Southern Western Hemisphere, crossing all the way to Canada's Northern Western Hemisphere." For the first time of my existence, I am contemplating such an indescribable view of the Andes high mountains covered with perpetual snow, nothing short of fascinating to say the least. It brought me great memories of those times while going away on vacation west of Bogota City, about one hour traveling by automobile, one was able to sightsee into the far distance some of the tallest mountains, with a white cape of snow, as it was always described. Now I am so thrilled just to be so close to them, the glass window is the only obstacle, preventing me from picking some snow. The airplane is traveling between the mountain corridor side alleys, incredible indeed, to say the least, quite a remarkable accomplishment.

There is not a question about giving a well-deserved credit where it fits, to the pilots, for taking such a delicate technical task of formidably maneuvering along the mountain's perilous established route with destination to Medellin, the second largest city in Colombia, where the first designated stop will occur. Alas! All of a sudden, the crew officers are announcing the latest official report that we shall be getting ready in position for landing within 20 minutes time. The stewards are going across the alley to double check that all passengers are following the instructions accordingly. Weatherwise, one could not ask for anything better than such a clear day where one could see forever, sunny, no wind factor reported at all, one great terrific contribution from Mother Nature. Just like a great miracle, as we approach into proximity to, and are ready to process our landing in, Medellin City, it is becoming more visibly majestic looking.

Little did I know that someday I would be at the tragic scene where 24 years earlier two planes had collided carrying some famous personalities from the entertainment world, renowned Tango singer and Argentinean actor Carlos Gardel and his musicians, along with a Colombian native Mr. Samper Mendoza, a young pilot, very popular and likely among the high society. The two planes collided on the runway according to official witnesses. One plane was apparently safely landing and the other plane under Mendoza's command was running on the runway ready to take off with destination to the city of Buenos Aires, Argentina.

There was only one survivor, a member of Carlos Gardel's entourage. Everyone else perished under a tremendous smoke fire, bodies burned beyond identification. My mother used to tell us that when she was a younger lovely lady and living almost three years in the city of Buenos Aires, she never had the joyful opportunity to meet her Tango idol. However, many years later, after she was already married to my father, pregnant and expecting the oldest of my brothers, she went to see him coming from his last presentation in Bogota's prestigious Colon Theater at the main avenue where he would be crossing to his destination, the Techo Airport. She told us that he was waiving to the crowds along the avenue in a farewell spirit. Needless to mention how excited my mother was to see him. Two days later came the tragic news about the airplanes' crash collision. Undoubtedly a sad moment all over the World; Gardel, the Tango king, was beloved by fans from all walks of life. My mother went into deep seclusion crying, and close to having a miscarriage, and had to be sedated. My father was to bring her pictures, newspaper information, whatever came out of the media. That was the story I heard, my mother's description of the legendary singer's fatal fate.

One hour after we landed at Medellin's Airport, and after picking up new passengers, we are instructed to take access back to the airplane where the crew is waiting to start final preparation. It is hard to believe that within hours since I left my original departure from Bogotá, we are now in the motion of a second take off departure with destination to Panama City in Panama, Central America. According to reliable official travel time estimation, the Airplane will be arriving at Panama City International Airport within two hours the most, considering the excellent atmospheric condition at present time. Good memories I am taking from Medellin, a remarkable modern City with spectacular climate and great hospitality, yes, indeed.

Here we are, ready to prepare for landing and I am looking through the window to take a view of this famous place where history was witnessed, the Panama Canal, one of man's mightiest engineering projects. Connecting the Atlantic and Pacific oceans, it was an astronomical financial adventure. It resulted in fatalistic human labor casualties, men's weaknesses succumbing to a mysterious infectious disease. It was later discovered to be caused by an insect, better known as the Malaria Mosquito plague. Incredibly devastating, discovered in the region then by the late Theodore Roosevelt, who was formerly United States President during the years 1896 to 1904 and Chief Engineer. In charge of such a tenacious project, the Panama Canal mission was accomplished despite previous attempts by other injunction nations, historically France and Colombia Republics. They could not sustain the difficulties from an inhospitable environment, in spite of possessing combined forces, targeting with firm determination to carry out such an almost impossible project. Treaties, careful planning, and financial investments were not enough factors to succeed. They finally abandoned the project, succumbing tragically to Mother Nature's forces under such strange circumstances. What a terrible devastating adventure in which these two nations pitifully became involved, a fiasco! How else could it be described?

I was unable to see the Panama Capital from above since the airport was built in the outskirts away from the city limits. However, I was very impressed with the beautiful tropical landscape lying ahead. For the first time in my life I was so lucky, contemplating such a magnificent scenario as the plane started to descend into the designated runway. A few minutes later after touching ground, and following diplomatic official procedures, finally, the moment arrives for me to set foot for the first time in my life on foreign territory at seventeen years of age. I honestly did not realize the magnitude of this historic event until next to me, my traveling companion brought me back to reality; I had been quite distracted by the jubilation of all the surroundings.

All passengers have been instructed to remain within the vicinity of the departure gate for about a two hour period during the plane's final mechanical inspection and refueling in preparation for our departure for the last leg of our trip to the destination city of Miami, United States of America. According to official sources, estimated flying time will be approximately five hours non-stop. In the meantime, while waiting for the passengers' last call to report to the gate, my seating companion suggests that we should go for a stroll since we shall be seated for such a long period of time and the plane does provide enough space for a walk. Also, she asked me very encouragingly if I would accept an invitation to join her for some refreshment at the restaurant. I thought it was very fond of her to invite me quite indeed. Being "a typical gentleman by trade" I offered to pay the bill. However, I was deprived from doing so; definitely she did not allow me to do so. Well I tried, insisting, but all in vain!

Finally, the plane is standing at the runway ready and waiting for control tower officers directing the departure time to take off straight up into the sky. I am thinking about such wonderful unforgettable memories left behind since departing earlier today from Santa Fe de Bogota, later on culminating in my first mortal experience ever setting foot on foreign territory at Panama Republic, which not long ago was a former Colombian State. So far so good, what lies beyond is unknown. All of a sudden, the plane comes into an air pocket. At this point, my state of mind turns into panic, what a horrendous sensation, as if I was going to die. Right after, the airplane started experiencing some turbulence, increasing altitude, and partially losing control. Later on, it was explained to me that it was not an unusual incident, as a matter of fact, quite common while crossing the skies. My companion realized how I was trembling and asked me to keep calm for there was nothing ominous to be concerned about.

If there was something worth mentioning, it was the stewards' courteous service, the elegant silverware setting, and diverse exotic cuisine dishes, meals served well enough for a King's demanding appetite. Suddenly, after more than four hours traveling since leaving Panama, an announcement is coming from the crew cabin letting every passenger become aware that the airplane is crossing over Cuba Republic and soon starting to prepare for arrival. The time scheduled is approximately 35 minutes to begin the landing descent into Miami International Airport E.E.U.U. with final destination to New York Idlewild International Airport, presently known under its new name, John F. Kennedy International Airport in memory of the former President who was in office from 1960-1963. A victim of an assassination, conspiracy? Only time will tell.

Upon my arrival into Miami on January 20th, 1959, I learned of some recent news that created furor all over the world and is worthy of mention. On January 9th, the Cuban Revolution was victorious under Fidel Castro's leadership and his two comrades Roberto Cienfuego and Che Guevara (Argentinean National), both of them long time deceased. The other case was of a crash accident, which occurred on January 17th, involving a small aircraft during a strong snow storm carrying a well renowned rock musician Mr. Buddy Holly and his band. I was not familiar with, or a fan of his, otherwise I would have been terrified taking an airplane, especially during my first time experience traveling by airways.

Suddenly, far away on the Horizon, in the middle of nowhere, darkness has created an imperially notorious presence. The airplane guiding lights are the only source of visibility all around in the still of the night. Then a few minutes later by some inexplicable miracle, upon reaching city limits, lights start appearing, shining throughout. It is really a splendorous display of fantasy in front of us. My first impression is nothing short of stunning contemplation, such a fantastic panorama in front of us quite indeed.

At last, our final destination has been reached, and stepping into this promised land's solid ground, arrival time is approximately 8:15 P.M. The temperature is quite mild and breezy and I am feeling kind of weird. There is not a question whatsoever that I am physically, psychologically exhausted far beyond recognition, comparing myself exactly to a prizefighter coming out of the ring right after throwing in the towel from an agonizing battle.

Once inside the airport building, all passengers are given instructions to follow straight ahead to the Customs Office to comply with all the required legal identification documents, typical protocol whenever coming from a foreign land. Right before going into my designated booth I decide to take the opportunity to express my gratitude to my traveling companion with some touch of nostalgia, without realizing it was going to be the last time I would be seeing her for the rest of my mortality.

What a welcome I received from my relatives who came to the Airport to see me upon arrival, some of whom I have not seen in so many years. We are all laughing, kissing, and hugging each other, a typical brotherhood scenario. As soon as we accommodate the luggage into the automobile trunk, and make ourselves seated quite comfortably, my cousin Louis Augusto immediately starts driving in a moderate speed. We leave the airport exit behind, headed directly towards my Aunt Epimenia's residence which is located in Miami City Flaggers community, some 35 minutes away.

Although this is my first time traveling into this unknown region, it is obvious that I am becoming accustomed now to atmospheric conditions and the typical fresh air. I am breathing the aroma being expelled from tall tropical palm trees and the vast greenery around, although late night time has fallen upon us. The moon's shining light has been the major factor in all around clarity. As far as the temperature, it creates some warm comfortable satisfying weather-like rains. I am amazed for all the surroundings are so beautiful, just like having an incredible dream, to say the least.

Finally, we have reached the residence and my cousin Louis comes full stop by the alley leading to a garage. Everybody is given instructions to get out of the automobile before pulling the vehicle in for the rest of the night. I am quite impressed with the house style, a one floor level ranch model surrounded by a well-trimmed front and back yard, and a white color façade, which is found more commonly in warm climate environments. The inside distribution is particularly symmetrical with four typical bedrooms, living and dining room combined, three bathrooms, and of course a very cozy kitchen, and with decoration professionally done.

While relaxing in the living room I am feeling exactly like I am in front of a court house jury surrounded by relatives full of curiosity, anxiously interrogating me about relatives' and friends' statutes back in Colombia. I am really enjoying the full conversation among us, however, at one instance my Aunt makes a suggestion that all of us should retire to go sleep. She tells them that I may be very exhausted from this particular day, a long intensive schedule right after more than an eleven hours journey. Before retiring to my quarters, I express my gratitude for the time they have spent picking me up at the airport upon arrival, and such a terrific display of hospitality since we met, after many years of not seeing each other at all.

I must admit Aunt Epimenia was right, and myself as well, in accepting her advice because while lying in bed reminiscing about my long trip, I went to slept soon after. Little did I realize how exhausted I was, succumbing to incredible body fatigue.

Chapter 3

It is the alba of a new day and all of a sudden my cousin Louis enters into the room to wake me after a well-rested night. He greets me with a kind of guilt-like compassion, without other alternatives to choose from, since they already have scheduled this day filled with activities. This includes taking me all around the city of Miami and the world renowned Miami Beach, famous for having some of the most beautiful shores refreshed by the Atlantic Ocean, with crystal turquoise waters and a soft touch of an invidiously tropical breeze.

My first breakfast ever in a foreign land consisted of orange juice, coffee, and scrambled eggs followed by bread, butter, and jelly, and finally culminating with a delicious bowl of cereal. Honestly it is my presumption that any Royalty from the Highest Hierarchy dating back to eighteenth century would have been jealous.

Great Scott! Something funny happened as I was strolling within the premises. As I crossed by the bathroom, the door was open and what was taking place inside was visible to the naked eyes. Well I could not help notice my cousin Theresa shaving her legs in a very compromising fashion. Never before, in my entire life, had I been witness to such intriguing and peculiar innocent female procedure. I was a total stranger to this hygiene maneuvering performance. She handled this incident quite normally; I personally felt very embarrassed, therefore I did not want to confront her at all.

The day is ideal for any type of outdoor activity, therefore Luis and Aunt Epimenia take me for sightseeing around town. The weather factor was a perfect temperature ranging in the upper 70's, one of those typical days where you could see forever. As we travel throughout different communities and commercial centers, I cannot help to notice that I am becoming fascinated with the tropical greenery all over the city. Going across into Miami Beach, the water front view is something I have never seen before, simply spectacular to say the least. Finally, we reach the Atlantic Ocean shores driving along and contemplating some of the most impressive hotels and resorts erected nearby the beach. There was one in particular that I became so impressed with and shall remember for the rest of my life, the Fontainebleau Hotel. Perhaps the largest in the region, it was quite an imposing monumental structural edifice.

It is becoming late and time is almost running out for me to start making preparation to have the luggage ready to go to the airport for departure for the last stage of my voyage to New York City. This is the final destination where my older brother Roberto is waiting for my arrival to take me to his apartment. There, I shall be living for a period of time until my mother, brother Herman, and sister Maria Amparo will be joining us according to plan within a year or more, once they have been granted their E.E.U.U. Visas permanent residence status.

It is unbelievable that for the second time within the 48 hour time period, I am going through another ceremonial farewell. This time it is a little less emotional atmosphere, in comparison to the first departure from Bogota, perhaps because I am getting familiar with these rituals. All of a sudden I am given assurance by my relatives that in spite of the weather report as cold, and recent snow storms in New York City, I am going to enjoy living in such a popular world renowned cosmopolitan city. I am unaware of what is coming ahead; all I am familiar with is whatever I have seen in film projections on the large screen in Bogota City, my place of birth.

Once all the information has been submitted and the documentation is in order, passengers are instructed to remain within the premises until further official notice over the microphone announcing passengers to walk through the portable corridor leading onto the plane for departure. Alas! Since I do not speak or understand English, a good samaritan comes to my rescue and in my native language he very courteously explains to me what the announcement is all about. Likewise, turning around I do express my gratitude for taking his time to help me.

As soon as passengers are seated properly secured and ready for takeoff, the Captain welcomes everyone, wishing all aboard safe, smooth travel to New York City. The estimated flying time will be about four and a half hours approximately. Also, he speaks on behalf of his official crew, who are following last minute details, ensuring maximum comfort. Right after he finished, while crossing the sky, I finally felt physically exhausted. Grabbing a pillow and properly adjusting my seat into a relaxing position, once my eyes are closed, I completely succumb to falling to sleep for the journey's duration.

Suddenly, a stewardess is calling me in a sweet tender voice trying to wake me up, and instructing all passengers to be immediately prepared for landing! Following official orders to properly secure my seat, I decide to look through the window to take a glimpse into the exterior space. The airplane is still crossing over the metropolitan area. All I am able to see and to distinguish are the city lights, reflections that seem to disappear far beyond on the horizon. It is really an incredibly spectacular view from above.

The landing has been quite normal without any incidents. The time must be close to 11:00 P.M. and the airport building seems kind of deserted. I am strolling across corridors observing all around, feeling like I am away somewhere in a remote isolated territory. Finally, I am reaching the customs office department. The agents on duty are immediately requesting to double check that my documentation is properly in order, complying with the Immigration Department protocol for entrance into the United States.

By the time that I am taking a brief rest and stretching my anatomy, I am able to see my brother accompanied by a gentleman waving to me through a dividing glass wall. I am so excited to see him again after two years earlier when he left Bogota, coming to reside here in New York City. Once we pick up the luggage, he provides me with a sweater, a jacket, scarf and gloves, and he properly prepares with the appropriate attire and informs me how cold the temperature is. We quickly take the nearest exit door into the public parking garage.

Oh my Lord! My first impression dealing with cold weather was horrible, there was no other way to describe it. I really felt like I was walking inside of a refrigerator. It was probably worse than spending an adventurous midnight religious mission retreat at Monserrate Church, located on the top of the mountain above the city of Bogota under a strong wind factor with a cold temperature in the low 30's on the Fahrenheit scale.

Chapter 4

My first impression of New York City the following days after arriving was somehow negative to say the least. The freezing temperature typical of winter season, which I had never been exposed to before in my lifetime, created health complications since I was coming from a warmer environment. I ended up spending almost two weeks of recovery taking full rest, medication, and drinking lots of accolades.

It was a horrible sight looking at the subway elevator system running on the tracks above the street level, and the noise created by metal's friction just unpleasant to any sensitive ears. There was no other way to describe this barbaric sightseeing medium of urban transportation.

Another experience that I came across while going sightseeing in the borough of Manhattan occurred as soon as we got off from the underground subway system and came up into the street. I became quite petrified upon observing fumes coming from below the street level. I was under the impression that the city was in flames. Immediately after this unexpected scene, Roberto with a kind of compassion, explained that due to the fact there were so many underground viaducts vital to the urban city, they required a system of expelling fumes right up into the city exterior, a good definition to satisfy anyone in my situation.

I became very depressed whenever the occasion arose when I found myself in situations where I was unable to understand the native English language and the lack of communication turned into frustration. Eventually as time passed on, I finally did overcome such an obstacle, a triumphal victory after a couple of years, quite an effort and dedication indeed.

Ever since arriving from my native Colombia approximately 5 years ago, life in my new adopted country has been fulfilled with the tremendous result of positive expectations. This is the calendar year 1964, and as far as my family status is concerned, we all are legal residents fully reunited after almost a decade exodus from our former country. This began back in the year 1954 when my older brother Edward came to live with my Aunt Epimenia and her family who had already settled in the city of New York, United States, two years earlier.

During those early years while residing in New York City, I was able to accomplish several successful goals (like learning how to speak English and obtaining part-time work while completing my studies) with the moral support from my family, and God's divine intervention, of course! After some deep soul searching, my financial obligation forced me to explore some alternatives. So I opted for seeking a job during the day and continuing my education by enrolling in an evening high school program. Upon graduation in January 1964, I continued my education by attending evening classes in a technical institute, and on weekends taking related courses at the Brooklyn community college.

It is very important to mention, that "Cupid" struck my heart after having met a young lovely lady while we were still in high school. Our relationship continued for years to come, flourishing with great tenacity; it was a very solid romance with great future expectations. We really enjoyed sharing with gusto even simple things that made us happy. As time progressed and I became extremely involved with typical everyday routine affairs, my physical status started to feel the effects created by too much self-imposed pressure. I reached a plateau where life style habits started reflecting irregular signs untypical for someone my age. I was approached by family members and friends who quite often were expressing their concern of how skinny I was really indeed becoming.

Nobody knew then that these phenomenal physical drastic changes were major factors in the original of what was taking place. The answer would not be revealed until later on as time went on and after medical intervention. The seriousness of these symptoms would be an enigma that finally would be medically discovered after undergoing several series of tests. Looking back trying to trace any sign that could be beneficial to lead to the mysterious weight loss, my recollection made me realize that for some time after I had switched jobs, there were signs of fatigue, I was losing my appetite and feeling thirsty quite constantly. My nutritional plan was not appropriate for the constant weariness that my body, physically and psychologically combined, was sustaining on a daily basis.

During the early part of year 1964, in spite of the fact that my body frame was becoming fragile, I was still able to perform most of my daily routines without any impediment whatsoever. This was really remarkable, a miracle to say the least. Even though I was feeling well, my brother Robert arrived at the conclusion that it was better for my personal interest to seek immediate medical attention. Therefore, he referred me to a Hungarian doctor by the last name "Speed" whose professional practice office was located in upper Manhattan close to 82nd Street by the German Town city section.

Finally, the day has arrived for me to go for the Doctor's appointment, and I am having the pleasure of my girlfriend

Clemencia's company. It is really quite a relief, a tremendous moral support from her. The trip is at a fast moving pace filled with a sort of anxiety; I am looking forward to meeting Doctor Speed and listening to his analysis. In the meantime, we approach the corner of Lexington Avenue and 82nd Street looking for the right address. Before we realize it, there we are in front of the building's main entrance, walking into the lobby and searching for the Building Directory. At that precise moment the desk porter comes to our rescue, asking very politely who we are searching for, in order to direct us to the right office floor level. I give him Doctor Speed's address so he can assist us immediately. We are told to walk towards the elevator and get off at the 4th floor.

As we walk through the corridor I start feeling kind of uneasy; perhaps my nervous system is trying to send me some messages. In my anxiety to find out what my physical condition is, I am in limbo to say the least. Very carefully, we open the door to his office, and as we come in, a middle aged nurse welcomes us and asks, "who is the person afflicted" that must be seen by the Doctor. With a little bit of humor I indicate that Clemencia is the one referred for observation. This reveals that I am still looking well. Then it brings me reminiscent of that famous quote, "do not judge the book by its cover."

Right after I listened to the instruction for completing the entire history application, and filled in all of the information requested, I returned it to the front desk assistant and I am instructed to wait for some minutes. During this time, the Doctor is quickly reviewing my health history application and preparing all the procedures before getting ready to see me at last. Once I am called to walk into his private room, I make a request that Clemencia be allowed to join me after the main procedures have been done.

After undergoing medical observation and physical tests, he arrives at the conclusion that my case is a result of some sort of infection, therefore I must start taking Penicillin medication. In order to eliminate such malady, he also requests that his nurse take some blood examples from me.

In the meantime, while we are waiting for the results, Clemencia makes her entrance and joins us. She really enhanced the office room with her beauty and modesty, an attitude typically characteristic from a Latin American lady. As she walks in, displaying some sort of surprise and timidity, Doctor Speed's admiration for Clemencia is obviously revealed. Once formal introduction is accomplished, he becomes kind of distracted and his curiosity starts revealing beyond belief. I have the impression he has a crush on her. Anyway, who would feel otherwise with her adorable, innocent looks? As a matter of fact, he expresses to me how beautiful she is. Ah ha!

Once the consultation with the Doctor is concluded, I am requested to see the nurse and follow her instructions to make the appointments to come back for a series of medications that will be applied at the Doctor's office for some undetermined time period, until I show positive recovery signs. Only Our Lord knows how long it will take before that day comes for full recovery; that is my conclusion.

What a strange weary kind of feeling I experience on the way out of the building into the street; I feel some sort of relief and anxiety. It has been an ordeal with too much stress, the only remaining consolation in my mind is the doctor's diagnosis. It is a typical case of a viral infection, apparently nothing grave. Once we start walking we join the rest of the crowd, where the mass of humanity crossing at different paces, some of them coming and some going, seem just like typical ants carrying out their daily routine work endeavors.

It is precisely time for lunch, and being in the Yorktown area, we opt to stay around by choosing a typical German restaurant just to calm our appetite. The food was delicately prepared, enough to satisfy any King's or Queen's gastronomical palate for that matter, to say the least.

The days are passing on faster than anticipated, and time is coming closer for me to be ready for my second Doctor's appointment. I am really anxious, looking forward to hearing the Doctor's analysis of early stage results from the first Penicillin shot applied just a week ago. I personally have not experienced any side effects ever since the prescribed medication was introduced into my system. God willing, hopefully the results will be positive right after the first tests have been concluded.

The Doctor's facial expression is inconclusive; his opinion is that I am definitely going to need another couple of weeks before any sign of progress may start to develop. After three weeks taking my medication religiously, I start to experience strong symptoms, like feeling a sort of dizziness followed by a combination of weakness accompanied with some other mysterious negative side effects. It was then when my brother Roberto reached the conclusion that I was not showing any vital sign of improvement, but rather, my condition was worsening. At that instance, he personally encouraged me to stop seeing Doctor Speed. Then, reaching the most critical decision, he recommended that I immediately go directly to the neighborhood's Elmhurst General Hospital in Queens County, New York to the outpatient clinic center for a complete physical examination.

Chapter 5

For the record, it was exactly the last week of March 1964 when I woke up this particular morning. Right after eating breakfast, I left home walking directly to Elmhurst General Hospital. I was not really nervous, but rather looking forward once and for all to finding out what was the source for all the complications which were afflicting me and my precarious system, causing all types of internal anomalies, yet, leaving me still feeling physically strong.

Arriving at the Emergency Admissions Clinic, I am immediately approached by a security officer who directs me forward to the Lobby Registration desk, where a receptionist in charge asks the reason for my visit. Then she provides me with some information which must be filled out for medical record purposes before I may be admitted, indicating very clearly the reason for my visit. After explaining my situation, the receptionist requests that I sit down and make myself comfortable while completing an application with all the details pertaining to my personal health history records. Once done, I return the form and I am instructed to wait for the physician who is going to follow the normal procedures of Hospital protocol.

While still waiting for my name to be called, I become astonished when seeing such numerous patients being registered. Some whose conditions are critical are being rushed into the revolving doors beyond to the critical ward unit, which is what

I am told by nurses on duty. It is really a spectacle watching and listening to the announcements coming from the speakers above. All I heard consistently was the screaming and painful complaints from the poor victims, only God knows what is really transpiring in their intense agony. I really feel like I am in another World; that is my truthful impression. It has been such an eternity before my name is finally called. As soon as I proceed into the designated room there for the first time in my life, I am surrounded by foreign medical equipment. An Assistant Nurse welcomes me very politely with a pleasant smile, appropriate for the occasion. Perhaps, I thought, she is trying to create some sort of distraction by making me feel quite comfortable. At that precise moment she hands me a white robe. I follow her instructions to go behind the booth curtains, disrobe from my garments, and wait for the Physician on duty to come.

Finally! I am quite pleased to see the Doctor walking in with such an imposing elegance typical of his status. He immediately starts by introducing himself, revealing his background and expertise in the medical field, and place of origin as a Greek native. He starts with the typical standard medical procedure by asking me my nationality, present age, personal status, present occupation, etc. Held in his hands is the information that I had previously submitted during registration.

As he starts examining me thoroughly, he asks me if I have been seen by other physicians prior to this visit. My answer is firmly positive without any further hesitation. Then, he keeps silent for a while, I guess a few minutes, like he was considering the procedures they may have followed and whether the conclusion to which they may have arrived was a misdiagnosis. In the meantime, I excuse myself and go further asking him for an explanation concerning the seriousness of my anabolic state. I also ask him if my condition is a typical symptom of anemia, diabetes, or an allied disease.

While still undergoing observation, he looks very close under my eyelashes checking for answers. At that moment, speaking from previous experience, he reaches the conclusion that my case is not a typical symptom of Anemia or Diabetes, but rather a case of blood abnormality, better defined in medical terms as Leukemia, or cancer in the blood. Of course! It is absolute speculation since I have not yet been officially examined. Then he turns around saying to me that I am a young man, therefore, I shall be psychologically strong. He encouraged me, kept me calm, and encouraged self-control as much as feasible. Why? Because he knew there existed the remote possibility of a cure that could help me recover from the disease if receiving the proper care and a little dosage of luck; a combination that brings a positive result in the end, after all.

As he excused himself walking briefly out of the room, I instantly turn my head looking up with concentration, pleading to the Holy Virgin Mother Mary that I am ready to accept my destiny whatever Her Holy wishes may be. Preparing myself for the ultimate, keeping my profound faith and the legacy that my beloved mother inculcated in me since childhood. What a wonderful spiritual gift bestowed on me; no doubt it was the greatest of all.

Upon returning into the room, the Doctor advised me that for my own sake I shall immediately be admitted to the hospital at once, considering the serious state and gravity of the situation. He gently wishes me the best and I reply with positive expressions and immense appreciation. Little did I realize, after such a brief encounter, that it would be the last time I shall see him for the rest of my life's existence.

Before being taken upstairs, I am requested to remove my garments and deposit all my belongings into a tagged heavy duty plastic bag that will be kept in a designated safe location until I am officially discharged from the Hospital. I am instructed by a nurse who is following orders to sit in a wheel chair, and then start our journey by taking me throughout the corridors directly to the elevator, then straight up to our destination on the 6th floor. By the time we reach the floor level, I ask her numerable questions. Perhaps, I am becoming too anxious, curious about what I will be going through.

Suddenly, the elevator door opens and a good samaritan allows us to exit first and my first impression observing the panorama in front of me is that it is amazing! This is the second time I have been admitted into a hospital institution; the last time, if I am correct, goes back more than a decade ago in my native country when I was almost eight years old. What a difference it was then.

In the meantime, while crossing the corridor, I take notice of how congested the place undoubtedly is, a madhouse. There is a line of beds against the wall, clear of the traffic of humans, and equipment, for that matter. Finally, the nurse brings me to full stop along the side of one empty bed where I am ordered to lay down and relax until further notice. Because my time of admission has been earlier than expected, I must wait before a semi-private room is available.

There is an incredible amount of commotion going on within the rooms and across the corridor; some nurses answering emergency last minute calls from patients experiencing some kind of physical agony, others, myself included, being transferred to newly designated vacant beds. Ceiling speakers are uttering a diversity of messages from the Central Station located half way on the middle of the floor. Those who are being discharged are accompanied by relatives or friends at such a sublime historical event. At that point, I arrive to the conclusion that watching this turn of events transpiring through the ward, screaming, yelling, staff personnel rushing, equipment being relocated or simply left for storage, is really a chaotic state, a crazy, mad place to say the least. My impression is quite similar to a typical scenario at any major airport, observing a mass of travelers getting ready for departure to distant places, or those who are just arriving physically exhausted, revealing weariness caused by a long flying voyage, vehicles creating tumultuous traffic delays, noise coming from avalanches, masses of people creating hysteria, a typical case of continuous locomotion, a chaotic environment at its worst stage.

After a brief time, I am finally assigned to this particular semi-private room that I am going to share with 4 other patients. One bed is still unoccupied, perhaps already on hold for someone who may be coming later. As time goes by, I start to make acquaintance with my room companions; we start by identifying ourselves explaining our personal background, and the reason for being there, which are the anomalies that are inflicting each one of us. I could not help to notice some of the uniform employees carrying meal trays and distributing them into different wards; I obviously came to realize that it may had been around the lunch time break, which happens to be the case quite indeed. It is late afternoon, and I still have not been seen yet by any physician, only the nurses who are starting to monitor my system and making the correct, adequate preparation for the next day ordeal ahead.

While I am contemplating the sunset in the distant horizon on a typical still winter day, by the window, and my thoughts are reviewing my first day's impression at the hospital, all of sudden my beloved mother and some of my brothers make their entrance into the ward. I am so happy to see them, and once they greet me with such a tenderness, I start immediately talking to them about what has transpired ever since early this morning after leaving the house directly on my way to Elmhurst General Hospital, which is located nearby in my neighborhood. As I am explaining some details to them, suddenly I become excited, extremely happy, and overwhelmed by seeing Clemencia, my girlfriend, accompanied by Helena her mother, and her sister Gladys, arriving at the room where some sort of emotional turn of events is starting to develop. However, everybody present is trying to maintain composure quite firmly; obviously it is not appropriate for any visitor to express the typical sort of compassion and sadness in front of the patient. Later on I came to realize why it was so important for anyone to keep their composure overall.

Since I would be undergoing a series of tests and some internal exploration the following day early morning, my relatives and friends were instructed to leave the premises in order for the nurses to start preparing last minute details concerning my physical cleaning and overall data. This is the first night in years that I shall be sleeping away from home; the infirmary rules are that all patients' room lights will be turned off at a determined hour, that is just about 9:30 P.M. Before I realize it, my body is succumbing to the exhaustion of this particularly long day.

Alas! Somewhere close to midnight, a series of incidents are starting to develop. For instance, a patient trying to reach his bed pan accidentally drops it onto the floor creating an alarming result and as a consequence wakening almost everybody, some of them yelling and screaming in such an uncontrollable manner beyond rational behavior, believe it or not. Others are calling the nurse on duty for an emergency perhaps, or any variety of reasons, some of them justified, and others just pure nonsense. I arrive at the conclusion that I am probably registered mistakenly to a wrong infirmary ward; there reigns an atmosphere of a typical mentally crazy institution just because of one single incident. Cursing among nurses and patients has become the order of the night, to say the least. Finally, after an exhausting verbal royal battle, peace is at last accomplished, and those involved in this fiasco reluctantly retire back to sleep in a sheep-like fashion.

All of sudden I have been woken up by the early shift nurse, who will be in charge of following the appropriate post-medical prerequisites. Once all procedures have been properly coordinated, I am supposed to be transferred back to my room where I shall be continuously under observation, waiting until further notice when the Doctor will dictate whatever is my official diagnosis, and then systematically apply adequate recovery procedure orders. I have not had breakfast at all and I am starving. Having said that, my lunch is going to be a well-balanced meal, as I am being assured by the nurses on the floor.

Later on that afternoon, right after eating my sumptuous lunch while still resting and watching television, I am greeted by some medical staff members, whose mission is to start immediately getting me ready for a high dose of blood transfusions. I must take these in order to counterbalance and strengthen my weak system, perhaps resulting from being exposed to toxic chemicals at work. Or worse, from being exposed to the wrong medication approach given by Doctor Speed during the time I was under his supervision, a typical misdiagnosed, medical case. I am advised by the medical staff that I should try to be aware of my arm, to keep it away from having any contact with my body even while still sleeping. Everything sounds comprehensible, however, at that very moment I become confused, wondering what I am going to go through once I fall to sleep. Upon consulting with them, their wisdom's reply is that I should try my best possible way to comply with this, and that the night staff nurses will be continuously monitoring the blood apparatus, observing that they are functioning properly without giving any margin for error, and responsive if anything negative suddenly develops.

Early in the morning the following day, I woke up experiencing some sort of discomfort. My right arm was still in a straight position since the night before when I went to sleep. I was informed by the nurse on duty that once the Doctor has seen me, she would proceed disconnecting the blood transfusion apparatus immediately from my arm, which she did indeed without hesitation upon getting the official approval instructions. What tremendous relief it was indeed, after spending the entire night holding my weak arm in a straight position. Somehow I was very lucky that no disaster occurred throughout the night while still being in a pitiful precarious position.

After a while, a tray is brought in and left on my rolling table, displaying a succulent breakfast fit for a king. I am not being sarcastic for expressing myself in such a manner. Let's be realistic, if you are extremely hungry, anything, even rocks, can be delightfully tasty!

My second day at the hospital is starting under an intensively busy schedule. Primarily, the doctor's round visit, taking prescribed medication throughout the day, a second physical examination plus X-rays to be taken, and the first blood transfusion results. A doctor's team is coming to examine and evaluate how much progress I have accomplished so far since I was administered the first blood transfusion. Alas! Later during the day, I have been informed that they have officially reached unanimous agreement upon positive results, therefore, another blood transfusion would be immediately administered.

It has been a very pleasant experience meeting the doctors who will be supervising every single detail concerning how I am reacting upon the transfusion, as well as some of the preliminary medications that I am taking to stimulate my fragile anatomical system and bring a sort of high degree level immunity to my system, therefore, preventing any critical infectious condition while I am still under that scheduled part of the recovery period.

By the third day at the hospital, I am starting to show remarkable improvement and positive physical signs. My appetite is turning gargantuan to say the least; I have gained some weight, my appearance is becoming everyone's talk of the town, as they say. I am feeling great after such a prolonged ordeal. The Doctors who have been involved with my quick recovery are more than optimistic, however, still cautious, being aware of the major magnitude of illness with which I have been affected during a long period of time for which only Our Lord really knows the outcome. Psychologically, I am feeling extremely comfortable, and quite determined to overcome the almost impossible dream's recovery.

On the fourth day I am starting to show good healthy signs. I am informed by the medical staff on duty that this is the last day I am receiving blood transfusions, therefore, they will apply some effective antibiotics to keep my body's system free from any possible contagious bacteria. It is terrific to know a prompt recuperation is in sight.

Some of my ward room companions are joking around saying that I have been transformed into another creature due to the fact I underwent too many transfusions. Perhaps some of the blood pints were donated courtesy of Superman; that is what they speculate and I go along with their hypothesis as long as it makes them happy. Ever since that first night of commotion, which I shall remember for the rest of my temporary life on this planet called Earth, so far so good. I have been feeling energetic and honestly extremely thirsty. Having said that, my digestive system would gladly welcome a pack of "cool beer," no doubt about it.

Something that I observe during visiting hours is both soothing and extraordinarily stimulating to me. Watching masses of visitors precipitate across corridors looking for relatives, friends, and acquaintances who like me are undergoing all types of physiological malfunctions makes me compare this scenario to a pilgrimage to a Holy Place, where anxiety, desire and confusion is the order of the day, that is my own observation indeed.

The end of my first week since I was admitted to the hospital back on Monday morning, has been endowed with a full remarkable experience. Never before in my life time have I gone through so many numerous ordeals; every single day and hourly schedule encompassed my way to a better future time ahead.

Chapter 6

Towards the end of the first week at the hospital, the Doctor's team who have been investigating my health condition have officially reached the correct diagnosis. In my particular case, symptoms have been declared as leukemia, a typical blood disorder that affects mostly children, and young men as well. During this time of events, I am introduced to a middle age foreign Doctor, by last name Vacca, who is originally from the Philippines. She is an intern specializing in oncology and allied diseases. She is my head-bed doctor and all major decisions would be subject to her professional determination.

My brother Robert has had a private personal consultation with the doctors who have been supervising my health's latest state. He is very much concerned upon listening and becoming aware of the real seriousness that I am confronting by the latest official conclusive diagnostic report. He is advised to seek professional advice by going directly to the hospital's Social Service Department and speak to someone who may be familiar with this type of case, since this is financially going to represent a remarkable expenditure. Immediately, it will require urgent relocation into another major hospital specialized in cancerous or allied diseases in order to receive proper care for what will require undergoing a series of treatments over a long period of time with remote expectations for complete recovery. Perhaps there will be a miracle from above for this incurable disease. If it is God's will, amen.

Of course, I must clarify for the record that all the maneuvering done by Robert during my second week at the Hospital was successfully accomplished very much confidentially without me being aware or personally consulted on such a critical decision! Later on, right after being discharged from the Hospital, Robert told me. He spoke to me about what confidentially transpired during that private meeting he held with the doctors where they discussed several proposed alternatives concerning my health situation. The decision called for undergoing a vigorous long treatment program at Memorial and Sloan Kettering Center, located by 68th Street and York Avenue in the borough of Manhattan. I was really surprised at such a turn of events because previous to this revelation, since my recovery had a miraculous result, I was quite under the impression that my health system had taken a tremendous positive turn as far as improvement was concerned. Little did I know about the whole truth behind closed doors; that was really my contention. Yes, indeed.

There are not enough words to express my deepest gratitude to Roberto for the entire time he spent, long days and nights, for my benefit. For his efforts and admirable dedication in support of enrolling me in probably the best research program to be found anywhere close within the metropolitan area of New York City. Time will pass by, however everything that has been done for my health benefit will always be perpetuated in my mind for as long as I may live. How lucky I am for being supported by such terrific, unselfish, and generous family members and friends, especially in times of uncertainty and despair.

A couple of weeks later, after being released from the Hospital, Roberto and I were on our way to pick up some forms at the Post Office in Astoria, Queens. Right after accomplishing our mission, it is precisely at that very instant as we step out of the place, when my brother takes the opportunity to inform me that some appropriate arrangements had been made by the Doctors to ensure continuation of my health care recovery. He said that being the case, what would ensue next would be to take me directly to Memorial Hospital in Manhattan later on after the holiday celebrations. By then, I would be enrolled and registered for a medical research voluntary program related to a diversified type of blood disorder known otherwise in medical terms as Leukemia, cancer of the blood.

As far as my case was concerned, a new revelation is no longer news for me to reckon with as I am by now accustomed to the unexpected. As a matter of fact, day after day I am teaching myself to be mostly tolerant, displaying good signs of patience, expressing humbleness, hope and acceptance to life's adversities as they come along. Something else that is extraordinary is that I realize that I am deeply convinced of an eminent religious spiritual approach to recovery. If it is the Lord's will, perhaps, the most important factor in desperate situations which involve terminal disease, then, I would obviously be devoted to practicing it, that profound faith, which is really considered a resource of last resort whenever a helpless situation may arise.

I have been so lucky by virtue of faith, which I have practiced with such perseverance throughout my life. Now more than ever it is going to play such an important role, while undergoing treatment, which could last for an indefinite time period. Obviously, I am immensely grateful to my mother who displayed tenacious dedication upon inculcating me with the power of faith, so long ago, ever since my tender years. She always reminded us constantly of the limitless benefits in keeping one's faith daily. She would frequently refresh our memories, producing one of her favorite traditional illustrations, and I quote her saying, "even if walking by the cliff's edge, be strong and firm with your faith, The Lord will intercede upon you."

It is that time of the year when members of the Christian faith gather together for the most sacred celebration in the Christianity calendar. I am referring to Holy week, which encompasses the period starting Palm Sunday with Jesus's triumphal entrance into the City of Jerusalem, followed by the tragic passionate events leading to His Death on the Cross, and continuing until Eastern Sunday, resurrection day, the greatest jubilee celebration of all, when Our Lord Jesus arises from the dead, fulfilling ancient Prophecies, Amen!

Once everyone is back into their daily routine, and grandeur of the Holidays have passed, Robert decided to get in touch with the Hospital Registration Department staff in order to verify day and time for admission to the center. All of a sudden, the day has arrived for me to start getting ready and adequately prepare my personal identification documents, which will be finally submitted for record purposes and double checked reviews. I am really anxious and looking forward to meeting the Physicians who will be in control while I'm undergoing experimental treatment.

Roberto wanted to avoid the early morning traffic rush hour into Manhattan, which can be chaotic most of the time. Therefore, for convenience, he decided it will be better off to travel early afternoon right after lunch break. Before leaving home, I do approach my Mother very tenderly, giving her a soft kiss on her cheek and close to her ear, whispering a very emotional good bye. She in turn replies with typical maternal kindness, words of hope, encouragement, and blessings, as well.

The commute into Manhattan represents no problems, on the contrary, it is a very smooth ride driving to our final destination, Memorial Sloan Kettering Hospital. As we are crossing Queens Borough Bridge, so many memories strike my mind. I reminisce of times when I used to go across, sometimes venturing into the unknown searching for entertainment or just simply familiarizing myself with countless attractions that a major Cosmopolitan City has to offer.

Once we have crossed Queens Borough Bridge into Manhattan we briefly encounter horrendous traffic by the First Avenue Exit. We turn right, leaving behind the bridge traveling directly Northeast towards the Hospital, approximately eight blocks away. So far so good, however, we then encounter some problems as we try to find a parking space in the vicinity. While driving around, finally, someone is getting into his automobile! And a few minutes later we find ourselves walking about two blocks to the Memorial Sloan Kettering Center, looking for the main entrance. We continue our journey straight ahead directly to the courtesy desk inquiring where we must go for my appointment. The receptionist very politely gives us instructions, right after reading the paperwork, which directs us halfway into the lobby where the elevators are located. From there, we go up to the 4th floor where staff nurses are already waiting to assist us in filling out additional questionnaires, prior to meeting the Doctors who will be strictly supervising any research studies done during the duration of my treatment.

While waiting for them to call us for our first official interview, I could not help notice the typical commotion created while the nurses were assisting some of the patients, especially infants crying upon being taken away from their parents. Obviously, these poor innocent creatures already were familiar with routinely uncomfortable examination procedures by doctors' staff. As well, it was almost incredible seeing the numberless patients from all walks of life, some of them looking cadaverous, very sick to say the least, physically afflicted by a diversity of Cancerous and Allied diseases.

Suddenly, we are instructed by a medical assistant that two Doctors are waiting to interview us. While on the way, as she takes us directly to the booth, my brother asks her approximately how long the interview would last since he is concerned with the car parking time limitation. She replies that it may run for about twenty minutes considering it is the first time, probably not more, and we shall be briefly subject to a sort of clinical patient evaluation based on family history health records.

As we walk into the designated booth, we meet two doctors whose personalities are admirable. With broad smiles they introduce themselves by their respective names, Doctor Bayard Clarkson, Chief Director of the Hematology department, and Doctor Alfred Gilbert, his Assistant Director. Doctor Clarkson is a United States native of Anglo Saxon background, tall, blond, possessing an extraordinarily imposing and distinguishable personality, perhaps in his late 40's. Doctor Gilbert, native from Montevideo Uruguay, is immensely involved in cancer research specialization under an extensive government exchange program and soon to become a Hospital Director upon returning to his native country. A very special and kind human, he is certainly blessed with attributes and an extraordinary humble personality revealing simple humane traits. I estimated his age to be somewhere in his 30's.

The interview was well coordinated. I myself was able to answer different types of requested questions, of course! My brother Robert intervened to fully expand on any necessary information, particularly, when encountering certain questions with which I was completely unfamiliar that concerned data pertaining to previous medical record history. Since I was transferring from another Hospital unaffiliated with Memorial Sloan Kettering Center, they definitely had to postpone administering any recommended medication changes until the entire official documents had been received and made available for their review. In the meantime, I would continue taking medications accordingly as prescribed and issued by doctors from Elmhurst General Hospital.

As we walk directly towards the Hospital exit, Robert invites me to join him for some coffee somewhere around the corner of First Avenue and 68th street, which I do accept with jubilation. While relaxing and enjoying our break after a long day with numerous agendas, he starts speaking to me about what is going to ensue next. In the following weeks to come, he says, concerning the research program to which I have been registered voluntarily, my present work insurance benefit would carry mandatory maximum statute limitations. Therefore, going beyond such limitation, in order to offset monumental long term care financial expenses involved, I shall be responsible for any additional uncovered medical expenditures.

Chapter 7

A week later, after having my official interview with Doctors Bayard Clarkson, and Alfred Gilbert, I receive a reminder message concerning when my next scheduled visit will be to the Outpatient Clinic. Sometimes while in meditation I question how many visits I will be attending, and the period of time for which this is going to take place, before I am informed whether or not there would be any chance for complete recovery. Well, I have reached the conclusion that only with the Lord's Divine Intervention, His infinitive mercy will set my destiny! Therefore, I shall continue to keep myself in high spirits, and in return for His goodness, a very strong faithfulness, letting his Holy wisdom choose whatever is in my best interest for the years to come. Having said that, it is up to me to establish a profound soul searching faith until the Lord would call me to His Kingdom for judgment day. It is definitely the only road to follow to expect a miracle recovery.

By taking the city transportation system, therefore eliminating the gargantuan, early morning commuting traffic in and out of Manhattan's borough, my first official visit to the outpatient clinic could be described simply as without any delays or incidents, exactly like I had planned. A typical city day exists where human masses become entangled while rushing to a particular destination. It is somewhere around 9:00 A.M. as I am arriving, entering straight ahead to the Lobby's entrance on 67th street. Continuing forward directly by the elevator area where it will take me to the 4th floor level, I am ready to be seen by Doctors and the medical staff team.

Right after undergoing typical normal physical procedures, a middle aged nurse asks me to follow her into a designated booth where once entering through dividing curtains, I am very much pleased to come across familiar faces, Doctors Clarkson and Gilbert. Also, there is a young nurse whose characteristics would best be described as someone who comes from the Old European Continent, very gracious and sweet vocal tonality, attractive and feminine as well, quite strong attributes to say the least.

Since this is the first official visit to the Hospital's Outpatient Clinic, I have been informed by the Administration Staff members that considering the seriousness of the case I have been affected by, perhaps a terminal disease condition, I may have to start undergoing a series of rigorous physical test examinations in order to determine what type of blood disorder is affecting my circulatory system. Therefore, a bone marrow exploration test scan will ensue next. Later on, while being interviewed by the doctors, once again they emphatically reaffirm the urgent importance to do bone marrow scan sequences on a regular basis indefinitely, as it may be necessary for the research analysis study. Thus, every time I come to the Outpatient Clinic for regular appointments I shall be subject to their grace until further notice.

After discussion of this conclusion, the assistant nurse approaching me delivers the appropriate instructions and hands me almost simultaneously a clinical white colored robe. Then she indicates to me the booth where I'm supposed to remove my garments from waist up, as well as some other items I must place within the appropriate designated area for my comfort and proper safety. To be honest, I find the robe kind of funny looking, however, there is no other alternative but to wear it. After all, I am not here for a Fashion Show at all, that is my assumption anyway.

As soon as I am fully prepared, they ask me to lay down and stretch my body in an upward facing position. In the meantime, while I am still waiting for the unknown, the nurse is already setting out a variety of medical instruments required to follow normal clinical procedures. Once everything is ready to start, Doctor Clarkson's hand is holding a hypodermic needle filled with a sort of anesthetic fluid. Squeezing some drops, he then mentions that I shall experience some minor discomfort when the fluid is applied directly on the chest bone in order to eliminate any acute pain when subsequently screwing in the interlocking component device. Properly spaced and seated to accommodate the 4 inch long needle that penetrates through a hollow center space, once the component device is ready, and the needle has reached the bone marrow requiring penetration, then, a standard hypodermic is directly connected into the component system device. Once all is ready, the doctor will extract blood from the bone marrow, directly transferring some of the blood into a hypodermic free from foreign fluid materials. When the blood specimens are collected, they will be sent immediately to the Laboratory for analysis.

While the procedure is in progress, I am becoming nervous in spite of receiving assurance that it is "pain free." I am still feeling so damn nervous that my only controllable alternative solution is looking straight at the nurse and pleading to her with an innocent request to hold my hand, which she does while gracefully expressing a great deal of compassion. In the meantime, those present created some spontaneous laughs, a very humorous circumstantial turn of events. Needless to mention that it brought me instant temporary relief, until the Doctor underwent the last procedure stage. At that very moment, I felt an excruciating acute pain that seemed to last forever.

Once everything was done, and right after taking some rest for about an hour, I found myself walking out of the Clinic carrying the next visit appointment slip instructing me to be back within 2 weeks.

I start strolling away from the Hospital's main entrance going south directly to the corner of 67th Street where I shall be turning right heading west towards the Lexington Avenue subway station to take the rapid system straight to home in Woodside, Queens. Great Scott! Upon approaching First Avenue a message immediately strikes my mind making me realize that I am not in any rush to be back home on time. Therefore, I shall take an opportunity to stop by the Catholic Church located at the corner of 66th Street and First Avenue to pray in solitude and express gratitude to my Lord for all the blessings and numerous favors that He so generously has bestowed upon my body and soul during all these precariously difficult times that I have experienced, while partially recovering from such a terminal disease. How long will I have to endure the side effects? Is there any remote possibility of coming out of remission, for how long, and what are the odds of a sign of development of a positive cure? Those are the precise questions that continuously are haunting my mind. One factor is definitely for sure and that is, my destiny is in God's mandate, Amen!

Life is really strange as it is, I wonder how many innumerable times that I may have crossed in front of this Church, however, it never occurred to me go inside for meditation and the Lord's visitation. Sometimes I arrive at the conclusion that for as long as one is healthy, enjoying whatever life has to offer, especially rewarded with mundane pleasures, a typical tendency for us humans as rational animals, is to forget the spiritual values and moral obligation resting upon Almighty God, including all those requests He continually listens to from us from day to day. The irony of life is that many times we revert to our Lord whenever time of crisis arises, finding ourselves desperate or hopeless, unable to confront the situation and solve our problems per se.

What an emotional moment is just about to occur as I make a firm resolution to stop in front of the Church. I start climbing up the concrete steps that lead into the Church's main entrance that can be better described in architectural language as having a Gothic style, which I find majestic and quiet, appropriate for a holy Sanctuary. A pair of lovely hand knobs attached to each door›s side is creating rich brilliant contrast to say the least indeed. As I pull the door open and go halfway inside, I become so impressed with the meticulous interior design, glorious decoration, besides an ambiance of Holiness, a perfect sacred praying ground.

Once inside, as I continue strolling forward towards the altar's front and the door behind me is slowly closing, I find myself in a different world. All around is complete silence, the city's outside traffic noise and the human congestion is not to be heard anywhere inside at all. My impression is just fascinating. I cannot help but notice additional alternating altars decorated with statues representing beloved Saints whose sainthood life legacy during their existence on Earth was recorded for future generations to come. Somehow, their rich spiritual contributions have no parallel in human history.

Meanwhile, as I am searching and becoming familiar with additional altars, my heart starts experiencing a great deal of jubilation since I am very lucky to come across Saint Anthony, my favorite one, whose altar is engulfed with numerous light candles, offers and petitions from faithful believers like me. Immediately, I bend on my knees and start offering prayers, asking him to intercede the Lord for His blessings and piety for as long as my short life span would be on Earth.

It has been such a wonderful experience, quite rewarding, filled with great expectations right after paying thankfulness and homage to Lords' Virgin Mother, and my favorite devoted Saint Anthony who has been my chosen Patron ever since childhood as far as I can recall. There is a rewarding feeling of satisfaction upon spending gracious time completely in solitude, praying to the Lord, Almighty. Amen.

All of a sudden I find myself walking at a fast pace joining masses of people who are probably coming out of work early. I cannot help noticing that some of them are physically exhausted, revealing a typical reflection, undoubtedly resulting from a long working day. Once coming inside into the station, all the hustle, pushing, and rushing from commuters trying to reach their final destination is really tough for all among human masses. I utter some words in discontent, like "welcome to the real World," after watching this scenario.

Later on that night before retiring to my chamber, I did experience a bit of discomfort. Most likely this was related to the effect of the dissolving liquids produced by the anesthesia, and the pressure set by the doctor into my center chest bone consequently creating sharp pain directly in the incision area, and followed by headaches.

Chapter 8

Ever since I started going for weekly appointments at the Outpatient Clinic at Sloan Kettering Center, which is annexed to the Memorial Hospital complex, the time has run smoothly without encountering any sort of complications. Consequently, I have become quite familiar with different itineraries, the governing Cancer and Allied floors' patient ward clinics, visitor and patient reception areas, and the cafeteria for hospital staff members, patients, and visitors, as well. Also, a private restaurant facility strictly used only by physicians and the medical elite members. If someone would ask me what impression I have concerning the Hospital's complex administrative system I undoubtedly would reply without any hesitation indeed, by describing it as a principality within the confinement of a major city. It is run by an administrative body starting from the highest elected Hospital Director in charge, and descending down to janitorial maintenance staff respectively in a qualified order. The numerous departments and wards are equivalent to cities' boroughs and subsidized communities. And there is a complex series of corridors, stairs, elevators, and tunnels for the purpose of quick communication within different departments or strategic nuclear medicine ward facilities.

The month of June is hastily approaching, and thus the summer season, too. Meanwhile, my pre-mortem final days are supposed to be over according to the unofficial calculations made by the first Doctor who saw me back around March at the Elmhurst General Hospital Emergency admitting office. His estimation was solely based on my precarious physical condition at the time; odds for survival were about 3 months. Therefore, my life expectancy was coming quite rapidly closer to the end of my existence on Earth. My only consolation was to implore Holy Mother, and Lord, for a peaceful death and eminent departure from this world of ours to eternal everlasting joyful life in heaven if that was my Heavenly Father's will, to be sharing part of His Kingdom with certainty indeed.

There is not any doubt about the fact that my mother was right, precisely from the very beginning when I was struck with an incurable illness, advising me to have perseverance and to keep my faith firm overall. As my final date with destiny was approaching closer for my eternal trip, she always had much tenderness and encouraging words. She told me to keep constantly praying, pleading to Our Holy Mother to intercede for the last minute to peacefully depart from this world in acceptance and with humility and resignation for Our Lord's plan and ultimate decision, Amen!

Meanwhile, as time goes by, my days are filled with several agendas; thus, I am very occupied. I am just realizing how self-satisfying it is to follow the perfect direction taking the correct approach physically and psychologically, ignoring mundane matters.

One day, while on my way to do some shopping for my mother, I received a telephone call from my girlfriend asking if I could accompany her to Richmond Hill High School for summer school class registration. I gladly committed myself to join her, especially considering she was not geographically familiar with the location at all. I asked her to wait until the following day since I already had errands to do and she was very much pleased to accept my suggestion.

The following morning, we met by the 74th Street, Jackson Heights Subway Station, and took the E train to the Sutphin Boulevard, Jamaica Subway Station. Once there, we took a walk approximately five blocks away, transferring to the Jamaica Station elevator train, then directly towards the Richmond Hill train station. As we were traveling and enjoying being together, it really brought on memories that took me back more than five years ago after arriving from Bogota, Colombia, South America on January 20, 1959, when I first started to attend school at Richmond Hill High School since I was residing within the school zone district.

Come to think of it, it was not too long ago when I walked into the School accompanied then by Roberto. What a coincidence indeed! Now it is my opportunity to give Clemencia a tour of my own, getting her familiar with the school grounds and therefore, already preparing her for the first day of Summer school. I must admit being seriously engulfed for some minutes with a sort of nostalgia. Everything around was still identically the same, no major cosmetic changes in the structure itself. In particular, I may mention that I fell in love with the indoor swimming pool first time I saw it, great memories.

Since the trip to the school is quite far, I have opted to become Clemencia's constant companion as much as possible. It brings me joy being close to her. Besides, my mind is actively occupied with little time to think about major personal problems that are presently taking place as far as my health status is concerned. I arrive at the conclusion that it is another pleasant way of being distracted to say the least. Alas! She is so lucky that her summer class starts at exactly 10:00 A.M., therefore, we shall be commuting after rush hour, avoiding the early morning rush of human mass congestion.

As time goes by, all seems to be going in perfect coordination, and visits to the Hospital are reaching a cornerstone. The month of August is approaching rapidly; the summer school will be ending in a couple of weeks. And I shall be celebrating over five months since I was admitted to Emhurst General Hospital back on March 24th, when for the first time, I was initially diagnosed with a type of blood disorder better known as Leukemia in medical terms. Also, I must mention that by God's will, a miracle is taking place within me, after being given a projected short life span of survival by the doctors of maybe three months maximum to live.

Sometime towards the end of July, right after my regular visit was almost over and I was preparing myself to leave, I received a shocking communication from Doctors Clarkson and Gilbert. They asked me to wait for a few minutes; it was imperative for them to explain to me the reason why they were taking a new drastic course of action. They were going to completely stop my medication in order to evaluate my physical condition free of Chemotherapy's dependency. How long would I be able to survive without any symptoms or signs of disease recurrence? Only time will be the best judge. They give me assurance that if I go back into remission they will be performing all types of analysis. There would be a variety of research evaluation upon any negative results, following whatever development may arise as a consequence. A brand new chemotherapy protocol would ensue next, by administering the latest series of medication available for medical research. This would be the ultimate option for them in order to reach an official conclusive diagnostic approach.

During the first stage free of chemotherapy, I have been instructed to continue my typical daily routine schedule, doing what I have done so far prior to starting the new investigative research program.

Chapter 9

During the summer season, Clemencia and I have seriously become more romantically involved, especially now, after undergoing such series of events. I really feel a strong bond that exists between the two of us from the deepest part of my passionate heart. Love comes in many ways, but we consider ours quite sublime, very special to say the least. Therefore, there is not a time in our thoughts that we might even consider being separated ever from each other, not even a single day. Our mutual feelings are so profound that we sincerely wish to get married and start living together for the rest of our lives, until God takes us apart.

Summer season is almost coming to an end, and thus Clemencia's high school summer class program, as well. I have been involved with a diversity of projects keeping myself psychologically occupied, creating some sort of distraction which is quite beneficial, especially at this critical moment of my life.

I am seriously involved with practicing my favorite sport of tennis. However, my mother is not too thrilled about it, because in her natural instinct she does not like the idea of me being overexposed to the Sun. Besides, there is a crossing hot wave of inclement weather. She does not intend to discourage me, but she implies with a lot of emphasis for me not to expose myself to such atmospheric conditions for my own sake. She is quite concerned about the complications and serious results that may develop as a consequence. I did intensive related medical research by reading books, and magazines, or any pamphlets that encompass reliable information pertaining to my illness' latest medical reports.

On one particular occasion, at the beginning of September, as I was returning home from the bank after a long vigorous walk, I started feeling some typical side effects similar to those I already had experienced back when I was first admitted to the Elmhurst General Hospital emergency ward. As soon as I walked into my home, I immediately called the Outpatient Clinic to report recurrence of drowsiness and trembling feelings while I walked. Needless to mention, they did not hesitate for a minute to ask me to immediately come the following day by early afternoon, considering the state of seriousness involved. They went as far as to question whether I would need any type of assistance that they could provide under such circumstances in my travel to the Hospital. I acknowledged them expressing deep appreciation, and responded by telling them that as far as I was concerned at the present moment, I was able to commute by myself unless an impediment arose otherwise.

Considering the time that I was scheduled to register at the Hospital this early afternoon, since I was feeling just fine, my final decision was to leave home about 3 hours earlier than usual. Therefore, I should have enough time to roam by large department stores around Fifth Avenue, just trying to keep my mind sort of distracted from all complexities ahead that were soon to develop. It was like taking gargantuan steps beyond into the unknown, but not really focusing on the unpredictable.

As soon as I arrived in Manhattan, all was going well until I started to walk inside of Korvett's major department store. As soon as I approached the automatic escalator which went to the second floor level, I instantly experienced a strong touch of dizziness followed by extreme lower torso weakness, reaching a critical level of almost no sensitivity. At that precise instance, I had to seek stability, holding myself against the escalator handrail. Something I remembered during the incident caused me to reach the conclusion that the store's fluorescent lights were definitely a determining factor since the store's illumination system was quite bright. It made me realize that in the past, I have always experienced some sort of physical discomfort or negative reaction to bright lights but exactly like my mother, who could have an accident but would never reveal any anomaly unless it was a serious case, I did not reveal this to anyone. I was kind of shy, besides, I did not want anyone around the store to know what physical reaction was transpiring in me.

I finally managed to step out of the store's exit, rushing straight to the Hospital. There is not a question about how I am quite nervously concerned about the desperate physical reaction that I am experiencing. Before reaching Memorial Outpatient Clinic, as I am walking hastily across town, there are not any more symptoms whatsoever. I just keep praying to All Mighty Lord to have mercy on me, and allow me to reach my final destination without further incident. Finally, I am coming into the Hospital experiencing some feelings of relief at last, for God's sake, Amen!

Once a room has been assigned to me, I am instructed to remove my garments and put on pajamas, then jump into bed and make myself comfortable while waiting for the Doctors to arrive. They will be performing a spinal tap test to determine what high degree of abnormal blood cells have been reproduced since the chemotherapy was stopped in order to determine exactly once and for all the correct diagnosis. As I am relaxing and watching some television, all of a sudden, I am distracted by the Hospital's white uniformed staff team coming into the room with one mission soon to be accomplished. That was to immediately set properly in order all the medical instruments that would perfectly be employed during this particular procedural test. This scenario obviously strikes my imagination; I really feel like I'm in the middle of a battlefield without any arsenal, sort of helpless, unable to defend myself facing such an impetuous army's arrival.

Considering the natural complexity involved in this crucial spinal tap test, I am given perfect assurance, mentioned very firmly by Doctors Clarkson and Gilbert that the entire procedure will be done within a reasonable time period. Also, they will try to minimize any discomfort that may surge while reaching their objective. This particular time the whole procedure will be performed by bed side. I am surrounded by the medical staff who are there performing as a team, ready to assist the Doctors if for any particular reason an emergency might occur, consequently resulting from an anatomic negative reaction. I am instructed to lay face down during the time the anesthetic is administered right into the area where an incision is done. A few minutes later my body must switch sideways, turning my back almost into concave position; that way the doctors will have more flexibility reaching the area while performing a very delicate partial penetration with a sophisticated screw intersection device component right into the bone.

Recollecting some of the major pain discomforts that I have previously sustained ever since childhood, never before in my entire life had I been subject to such an agonizing experience like the one I just went through while I was undergoing the spinal cord tap test. The tension was really uncontrollable, even at the moment the anesthesia was being applied, I was already feeling pain, not the soreness they mentioned. My body temperature rose to very high level and obviously my pajamas were completely wet because of sweating, of course! Needless to say, nurses came and changed the bed linen and I wore a hospital robe for personal comfort.

After having a light dinner, I was exhausted and immediately succumbed, falling to sleep throughout the rest of the entire night until dawn.

The following day, late in the morning, I had a pleasant visit from Doctor Alfred Gilbert, who personally informed me that there was not any further reason for staying another night at the ward. Therefore, since the complete test results were successfully accomplished, he would officially issue a formal discharge some time during early afternoon hours. I was very thrilled upon hearing the good news, and immediately called to my house asking if Robert would be available to come by the Hospital to pick me up and give me company on my way back to "home sweet home" indeed.

As soon as Robert arrived at the hospital he was advised to stop by the Doctor's office and speak to the assistant in charge, to listen to the latest communication concerning the nature of my case and test results and to know what would ensue next, after all analysis had finally been concluded. A week later, I was back for additional observation and an explanation of a long experimental project that I would be undergoing immediately, hopefully looking forward into the future for at least any remote possibility of coming into remission, thus partially recovering. I would follow a strict protocol of medication consisting of four different drugs, some of them extremely toxic, having strong side effects. I have been informed that once a month I may have to check into the Hospital and stay overnight for this particular reason. How serious would it be? Upon creating an unpleasant side effect through different parts of the metabolism, only as time progresses would it reveal perhaps a devastating end result to this ferocious battle against mysterious cancer elements.

For the rest of the week I was able to relax, although experiencing discomfort precisely on the area where the spinal cord tap test was performed, creating such agonizing deflexed results, that my mother advised me to take pain medication. However, I decline this. As far as my appetite was concerned, there was not a major change and I was successfully carrying out all of the typical daily routine activities which gave me so much satisfaction indeed.

Chapter 10

The month of September is upon us and the school system will soon be opening the doors for another educational year. Therefore, I must call my girlfriend Clemencia to touch base with her, since I have not seen her for almost 2 weeks, as she must be getting ready to continue another year at Newton Public High School, located in Elmhurst, Queens.

The following week, after the spinal cord test was successfully done, I did return to the Hospital for the results of the analysis. They discussed crystal clearly the leading major factors, as well as post-research conclusive evidence later found, that the Doctors used to reach a correct diagnosis. I had to be present to become informed of the new protocol of the revised medication approach. Therefore, I will resume taking medication consisting of two previous drugs labeled Metrotoxethy and Valedium, combined with two additional new drugs (See Appendix for medical records), which are supposed to have an extremely toxic reaction among those patients who are sensitive to such protocol of medicines; very strong to say the least. Obviously, the end results were optimistic, however, the side effects were devastating to the majority of those patients, who eventually would ironically succumb to the combined medication rather than the disease itself. For some researchers, this ultimate decision to continue applying a new diversity of chemotherapy would definitely be rewarding for their tireless research studies. Their efforts in trying to control or discover the cure for this endocrine mortal disease, and finding a normal basic balance by eliminating most of the cancerous cells, would be a partial earth-breaking success fulfilling long overdue expectations for excellent end results.

A week later, after having undergone a major spinal test and with laboratory results turning out to be conclusive; the doctors were quite satisfied with the research's end results. Thus they have arrived at a unanimous agreement, solidly based on the latest clinical reports, that I should immediately undergo a revised approach by taking a combination of drugs all at one time. This was precisely after two months earlier, when doctors decided to interrupt the chemotherapy strictly for experimental observation during a limited time period to establish what my body's reaction would be while free from medication. My body's first reaction for the first four months was feeling immune from any side effects or negative symptoms. This was a perfectly normal reaction taking into consideration the long span of the drug layoff period. It completely reassured full self-confidence indeed, physically feeling stronger now and better than ever. After this period of time, I came out of remission.

A new chapter in my life was ready to be unveiled. As soon as doctors assigned a new protocol of medication, I was properly informed that it would probably be considered perhaps the last alternative to hopefully fighting this terminal disease. However, there would be some repercussions that might develop into serious side effects as a consequence from some of the strong medications' high toxicity that my system may not be able to tolerate. How would my body react to these medications? What would be the length of time of this treatment before any positive signs resurfaced? Well, being purely realistic, nobody has the crystal ball for a magic answer; but only God Our Lord does surely enough indeed.

Chapter 11

As time is going by at such a fast pace, my body is responding extremely well to the medication, so far without any side effects, a sign of great relief to say the least. I am now developing a great source of confidence. I am also developing an urgency for returning back to work realizing that it has been such a long time since I was temporarily forced to quit due to the poor state of health that I was then undergoing. My determination to find a job position is beyond belief. I am filling out dozens of applications, delivering them personally and immediately, going through news media employment classifieds, answering the ads, making calls requesting appointments, etc. I do really feel like I'm experiencing being involved in a free-for-all Battle Royale.

Alas!, a couple of weeks have passed by when all of a sudden, for my own consolation, I do receive a call from one of the previously listed ads requesting that I come as soon possible for an interview. I am informed by the receptionist that there is an open job position available, and since I reside not too far from the Company's location, the personnel supervisor is very much quite interested, making a recommendation for me to have an interview. My response is obviously extremely firm; committing to be at the job place as soon as possible at their convenient time.

After going through my early traditional prayer's homage, and indulging myself in a well-balanced breakfast, I request of my mother her daily blessings precisely right before stepping out of our home. This is a ritual that mother taught all of us, brothers and sisters, since we were infants "not long ago" quite indeed.

Considering distance to the interview location, making a firm decision, I opt to walk having time to meditate, do my regular exercise, and mentally prepare myself for the anticipated interview already scheduled for today, September 21st, an invigorating refreshing late summer's morning. Surely enough, as journey distance is technically concerned, I have perfectly calculated timing for arrival, thanks to The Lord. I have no problem whatsoever finding the main entrance door that leads into the receptionist window where a young attractive lady asks me to take a seat and fill out additional personal information. Once I undergo the typical formality of filling out the application, to my delight, I am informed that I have officially been hired for the sought out position.

A couple of weeks later, while visiting Clemencia, she informed me her regular monthly menstrual cycle had already been altered for the second consecutive month, therefore, she was becoming quite concerned about this course of events. After some confidential conversation, we decided that for her own health reasons, she would undergo a complete physical examination, thus removing any doubts from our minds so there was no need for any more wondering what really was the case and origin of her natural complication. Since I already had become familiar with medical care help, I went directly to Elmhurst City Hospital seeking personal orientation. I finally met one of the social workers who was generous enough to provide me with a referral list of several doctors who were affiliated with the hospital institution.

Later on that week, after reviewing the list, we opted to select a doctor whose top qualifications and experience were excellent. Besides, he had been born in Cuba, and he was fluently bilingual, being able to speak English and Spanish, our native language. We surely arrived at the conclusion that it would be really advantageous to have a perfect, straight and clear communication with the doctor, yes, indeed. Therefore, he was our ultimate choice.

On our way to the doctor's appointment, somehow there prevailed a deep nervous feeling of ambivalence, obviously related to answers to unknown expectations. What would be the results of the symptoms? Once Clemencia had undergone the physical examination, since it is almost lunch time, we decide to stop by one of the nearby restaurants in the neighborhood to satisfy our appetite, relax for a while, and eliminate our anxiety, as well. Something we definitely agree on is that taking a brief resting period would become a panacea for the such complicated confusion we are experiencing at this very critical moment together, to say the least.

The makanna is already solved, now is time to start making adequate preparation, anticipating what will culminate soon in celebration of the holy matrimonial sacrament in months to come. Presently, time is our worst enemy, therefore I am starting to look for a place to live. So far, I am really optimistic that somewhere, somehow, we are going to find at nice clean place as close as possible to our relatives' home. Also, I am already preparing to purchase basic essentials that we are going to need when starting our first sweet home. Definitely, there is no doubt about the fact that it is going to be better described as a titanic mission to perform in such a hasty lapse of time. In God's will, with a little bit of patience and determination, all will be accomplished by dateline.

Canvassing around, looking for any shelter vacancy week after week, we have finally found a very cute intimate apartment, at an envious location not too far from mother's home site and Clemencia's family, as well. But most importantly, it is close to the

Catholic Parish which is just three blocks away, a short walking distance directly to the Church. A miracle by itself, to say the least, Amen!

In the meantime, I am receiving good stimulating news directly from the doctors concerning how effectively progress has been gradually accomplished while being treated under the latest protocol research program. Physically, I am feeling quite well, with a great deal of psychological optimism, even though it is still too early for the doctors to report any positive signs of disease being under control. They are very cautious, monitoring how I am improving since the latter week of March when I was first admitted to the Hospital. Also, I have been informed that of the four different types of medication that I am currently and will be taking, which will be administered within a month and a half, they may be quite toxic to my metabolism since the majority of patients have succumbed to typical side effects produced by the medicines. Only time will tell whether or not I shall be joining such a "distinguished" selected group. In the meantime, I am carrying on with my regular daily activities, hoping for the best to come.

Chapter 12

Considering the seriousness of the situation that Clemencia and I are involved in, not to mention the moral obligation and tremendous responsibility laying ahead with her pregnancy confirmed just recently, we have sought professional counseling. We have been referred by a social worker to meet a religious counselor whose spiritual approach, and his highly degree of University education, unquestionably makes him the perfect candidate to review our case. He is a very special Priest, Father Paul Cassaboum who has an impeccable command of the Spanish language. Besides, she says he is naturally gifted with a very good sense of humor and a humble noble soul. With such eloquent classifications, we reach a final decision by requesting a private appointment with the Reverend. A couple of days later, we are on our way to Our Lady of Guadalupe Church, located on 14th street and 7th Avenue, downtown Manhattan, where he officiates religious services as well as teaches in one of the highly well-known educational centers, New York University Campus.

It turned out to be a life experience interview, meeting him for the first time. We were extremely impressed by his unequivocal down to Earth personality, a devoted God's servant soul whose charismatic quality really inspired confidence, above all. We went through a full debriefing, explaining to him that we were looking to get married as soon as possible considering that Clemencia was officially declared being in the preliminary stage of pregnancy. We revealed to him that another urgent factor for such haste was that at present time I was being treated in a Cancer research program at Sloan and Kettering Center Memorial Hospital, while undergoing medical treatment for a terminal disease, better known as Leukemia.

Upon listening to the news and becoming aware of such a devastating illness, he directly addressed the issue to Clemencia and explained to her that statically the odds for my survival were practically none whatsoever. Therefore, it was not a basic reason for her to become married, solely because of her pregnancy. Rather, he advised her to reconsider and possibly reverse her decision; perhaps, that would be a proper approach to solve the present crisis involved. What ensued next? Once his advice was delivered, she responded with a high degree of determination and without any sign of hesitation, that even the thought of realizing that my life expectancy was so limited, statically speaking, she would marry me anyway in God's will, and that it would be her ultimate decision.

Later that week, we double checked the calendar schedule to set a date for such an important day in anyone's life annal. By important, I am referring to our wedding day Holy celebration event which would take place at 6:30 P.M. on October 15, year 1964.

There was some major complication while trying to convince our parents to agree for approval to our endeavor. We obviously realized that there was so much at stake, especially considering the condition of physical recovery that I am confronting now. Quite encouraging, ever since my life expectancy had been affected while battling this mortal disease, my destiny on Earth still is a mystery. Statically speaking, chances for survival are significantly and extremely reduced, the odds are similar to that of a suspended body supported by a thin tread. As far as financial estimating was concerned, the economic situation somehow revealed itself to be quite precarious to say the least. However, as time went by, together we cultivated a very strong bond based on faith and positive outlook expectations.

Some weeks later, after celebrating our Holy Matrimonial union, I gave the doctors and staff the great news concerning my new status as a newly married man. Needless to say, they really were hysterically laughing, followed immediately after by a mutual state of shock upon my personal revelation. Indeed, they thought at first instance that I was just simply kidding. However, upon looking straight at my natural face and perceiving my serious expression, they became somehow quite embarrassed and looking serious too, realizing that I was providing them with exactly the correct information about the disclosure of my personal news. What ensued next amongst the spontaneous confusion, was a call for my firm attention and their explanation of why, of course, they were seriously concerned with my present health condition status. Also the simple fact that I never disclosed to any of them my personal decision, failing to acknowledge them, before I catapulted this emotional chapter of my life.

November is approaching rapidly, the seasonal holidays likewise. It makes me ponder how fast this year is going away, as well. Precisely two weeks after our wedding, doctors have decided that I will be admitted to the Hospital for my first dosage of the long overdue dreadful medication. The doctors advised, with consideration for my job, that it would be best to administer the medication on a Friday so that if any uncomfortable side effects occurred I shall have the entire weekend to myself to recover from any complicated symptoms, if that was the case. The execution day has been unanimously preset for the following week, early Friday afternoon. I am instructed to register at the Hospital for admission, staying overnight. Alea iacta est, "the cast is set," translated from such an immortal eloquent statement produced by one of the greatest leaders that has ever lived in human history, and my greatest inspiration, and I am referring to Emperor Julius Caesar (76 B.C.), supreme leader, General of the Roman legions.

I am getting ready to make all the required preparations to stay overnight at the Hospital since I have been previously informed that this particular medication I shall be injected with intravenously for the first time has a notorious characteristically toxic result. According to statistical records of patients who have been exposed to this drug, the majority have had a strong reaction, succumbing to extremely nauseating symptoms, anxiety and convulsions, to say the least. It has been mentioned basically, and found quite conclusive, as well as described crystal clear. I am trying to psych myself into believing that in spite of it all, in spite of the real facts, that one way or another I shall be waking up victoriously from such super toxic applied medication. Ultimately, whatever the final result will be, I must overcome adversity, accepting reality. That is the bottom line.

Chapter 13

Today Friday, I am leaving earlier from work quite contrary to what is customary. As a matter of fact, I already had brought it to my supervisor's attention on a previous occasion that an important appointment was already set on my schedule amongst a very personal priority agenda. Therefore, somewhere about 2:15 P.M., Roberto arrives at my workplace just on time, as he usually does whenever committed to picking up anybody. No doubt about it, when it concerns punctuality he is very responsible, this is his typical trademark. How great is it to rely on someone who possesses those particular qualities? Having said that, a few minutes later, we are driving straight forward on our journey to the hospital where the doctors and medical staff are waiting for my prompt arrival.

I walk inside of the outpatient clinic to the admissions office and properly follow the protocol procedure. I am approached by a team of nurses who are taking me directly up to the 6th floor level where a single room has been assigned for my personal comfort, in case of any strong reactions developing during the administration of the newest medication I shall be undertaking for an indefinite period of time. Honestly, nobody has the slightest idea of the correct answer as to how long, this is basically the case.

Precisely around 5:00pm, while I am resting on my bed and watching the latest news on television, I am instructed by nurses to be ready for the medication which is to be administered. Medical equipment is set next to the bed with a plastic bottle filled with plasma, a liquid formula needed to fortify my system, hanging from the apparatus with a transparent thin extension tube attached to it, and at the opposite end, a hypodermic component device which is supposed to be connected to my hand's visible veins.

As soon as the procedure starts, I am told there will be a little bit of sore feeling as the needle is penetrated into the vein. By this time, I am completely terrified listening to their preview of the development. The satisfying news is that one of the nurses is consoling me by rubbing my arm with such a tender hand. Just a few minutes later, Doctors Bayard Clarkson and Alfred Gilbert make their imposing entrance into the room with a friendly smile, and very gently greeting salute. Needless to mention, my heart was engulfed with joy, fully satisfied with their presence. They really inspired much needed confidence in me, to say the least.

Upon final review and confirmation that the medical records met the criteria in order for them to administer the procedure, they continued to fill the hypodermic with a viscous drug liquid similar in color to Chinese sweet duck sauce, which later on throughout my life I came to detest because of the similarity in color. Every time I would be seated at a Chinese restaurant, my immediate request to the waiter was to infallibly remove the duck sauce away from sight; there was no question that I would instantly react negatively by developing an uncomfortable allergy to it.

Right before the Doctors walked out of the room wishing me a peaceful night, they instructed the night shift nurses to be aware of any convulsions or any type of negative reactions. They advised them to monitor my anatomy continuously, also to supply anti-nausea drugs to offset any violent side effects that may occur. These statements obviously anticipated a somehow disastrous result since this toxic medication seems to enjoy such a vicious reputation among the majority of patients who have been exposed previously to this dreadful drug.

Once the whole procedure is performed, I suddenly succumb to physical stress created by the ordeal, falling to sleep soundly. Somewhere around 2:30 A.M. to be almost exact, I wake up experiencing tremendous stomach discomfort, feeling a strong nausea reaction that never before in my entire life have I had any recollection whatsoever experiencing. A few minutes later, symptoms started to intensify more frequently without any sign of relief; quite the contrary, it turned very nasty, worse than ever before, therefore, forcing me to ring the alarm bell to request immediate aid from a nurse. It took just about a few minutes for one of the night shift staff nurses to rush into the room and come to my rescue. Upon seeing my stage of excruciating pain and poor physical condition, caused by my stubbornness from not allowing them to administer medication to combat the side effects, she takes hold of a hypodermic containing sedatives to control the strong reaction in which I was entangled. Considering the seriousness of the situation, she decides to release the intravenous device, leaving my arm free, thus, making it easier for me to somehow have enough flexibility and freedom to move. It was turning into a worse-case scenario accompanied by a visible physical exhaustion and severe stress previously not registered in my personal medical history.

Precisely at that particular moment of the night, while undergoing a very strong body contraction, with final determination I decided to stroll into the rest room where I spent a great deal of time releasing an almost uncontrollable saliva-like substance from my mouth. It did cross my mind that it would be extremely difficult to overcome such a horrendous ordeal may

I say. But then again, reminiscent of different experiences from other patients who became exposed to the same medication, and having listened to their own personal horrifying versions, I took profound determination that I would overcome all the odds some way, somehow, like they all had luckily survived such an ordeal.

The following morning, after I had spent over three lingering hours in the restroom, totally confined should I say by self-choice, completely helpless, physically exhausted, it was then again when I was able to recover from such a horrifying nightmare. Closing my eyes, allowing sleep to resume, having some decent time to go back to sleep, thus, recuperating from an insomnia state of mind and requesting that there be no disturbance whatsoever, except for any Doctor's valid medical reason to do so.

Somewhere around early afternoon, upon waking up from my prolonged dream, I was instructed to take a physical test, which was done diligently. Once the results were reviewed they were found to be positive, and I immediately received the good news from the medical staff on duty, who said I could be officially discharged, therefore, spending the rest of the weekend at home relaxing for prompt recovery.

According to the protocol research program guidelines, the next time I shall be taking this toxic drug it will be administered within 4 months from today. Great Scott! Now that the coming holidays are so soon just upon us, I can say with a great deal of certainty that right after overcoming the bizarre ordeal, that I shall be able to enjoy the festivities, of course providing it is the Lord's divine will, Alleluia.

Chapter 14

As we are approaching the holidays' celebrations and getting ready for perhaps the busiest time of the year, and as we are rapidly moving into the end of the year 1964 and preceding the new year of 1965 ahead, it is very important for me to seriously concentrate on practicing meditation and deep soul searching, to reflect on all the major chronological events that have occurred throughout this year, therefore, setting a new direction on my life. Incidental events that have marked an extremely important role, including drastic decisions properly taken in order to survive perhaps, thus, overcoming one of the most tragic ordeals that I have ever endured in my entire life. Not since childhood, when my mother had sustained an accident losing her balance while walking downstairs from the second floor level, had anything so catastrophic occurred. She was then within the stage of six months of pregnancy, but somehow, thanks to Our Lord's divine intervention, my mother's and my life were spared. There is no doubt about what our destiny was set out to be, which is surviving such an unexpected critical experience. It was a miracle quite indeed.

Once the Holidays were officially over and the mass euphoria created as a result, it was then my perfect opportunity to do some reflection dating back to early March, when I experienced some major issues concerning my state of health, very serious symptoms indeed. It was exactly 10 months since I was officially diagnosed with a rare type of blood disease, when I was consequently declared to have Lymphomatic Leukemia, based on previous statistical medical records and an expert team of Doctors. Upon reaching the ultimate decision, they unanimously agreed that I only had a period of three months to live. Chances of survival were practically null whatsoever, therefore, any remote possibility for any kind of recovery was non-existent indeed, according to the most reliable and latest medical research report accomplished per se.

That was then, but now I have really shown positive signs for a partial recovery, although still too early to declare success, which remains to be seen. To everybody's delight, I have been in remission throughout most of the time since I was transferred to Memorial Sloan Kettering Hospital Medical Center. Therefore, ever since my relocation, the odds are probably working in my favor. May I declare firmly with profound faith that undoubtedly in God's will, a miracle is in his sacred planning, my lord will be sparing my life for one divine purpose. Perhaps, I may have a major mission to accomplish while still alive, although considering myself such an insignificant unworthy creature from this existing world. How much more shall I have to endure for my missionary purpose on Earth to be revealed? Precisely only time will tell, as the years gradually will be passing away.

In January 1965, my first regular appointment to the Outpatient Clinic turned out to be quite interesting and delightful to say the least. It was such a great deal of pleasure just to hear that most of those patients who I personally met, and with whom I became an acquaintance during the last year in 1964, survived somehow, undergoing such a tenacious chemotherapy protocol research program, really a miracle indeed. My physical examination turned out to be positive, and laboratory results were completely satisfying after being reviewed, subjected to a criteria that was analyzed by medical researchers.

One of the most touching personal experiences I underwent during my first year at the Outpatient Clinic was when I was sharing the same floor level with the children's ward. I was often witness to a painful scenario, seeing some of the infants and young children becoming petrified whenever medical staff would approach the parents, taking them away for observation or physical examination behind the room's dividing curtains. Poor innocent creatures, they were screaming, calling incessantly, stretching their fragile arms, seeking dear ones to rescue them from the unexpected ahead, a touch of human lamenting, to say the least.

In spite of the fact that I have been basically in remission for a period of quite some time, which the medical records attest to, I still wonder for how long will this be going on? Enough is enough to such an uncertain future ahead; that is my deep soul searching speculation I may say, no doubt about it. Let me continue throughout my time with one enormous mission resolution, which is opting to choose a typical and normal kind of life just like all the other homo-sapiens inhabiting planet Earth.

Chapter 15

It has been such a delightful encounter meeting some of the patients who just like me have been afflicted with the same or allied diseases, thus, sharing similar experiences and therefore, establishing a common strong bond among us all. The friendly atmosphere that reigns by the waiting room is quite stimulating indeed considering the gravity, perhaps the certainty, concerning the near future; the months ahead embracing an unpredictable ratio to any slight opportunity for partial recovery, or survival, as it may be.

The beginning of the New Year was marked with a great deal of pleasure. Seeing most patients returning to their regular routine appointments I noticed something peculiar; they all were showing sort of a weariness on their faces, signs of exhaustion, perhaps an attribute as a result from too much partying during the recent holidays. My personal observation about immortality is: life is too short, therefore, why waste it, may it be merry and joyful while it lasts, quite indeed.

During the middle of the month of February in 1965, I was sitting by the Outpatient Waiting Room, waiting to be called according to the visit scheduled by my doctor, when all of a sudden, I was in a state of shock upon looking at this young lovely lady who I have not seen for quite a while being transported in a wheelchair pushed by a relative of hers. Since

I do not have a recollection of her name, in absence of her real name I shall apply a fictitious name, and identify her as Linda. She was looking extremely weak physically, in a cadaverous-like state; there was an expression on her face that was engulfed with sadness, disoriented, and ultimately resigned to the merciless disease. Remembering Linda from her previous visits to the clinic, she always had such an angelic natural look, besides a gorgeous facial expression gifted with a beautiful smile, unique and typical of hers that every time Linda made her entrance into the clinic, she did it with great exuberance just to say the least. Another of her personal qualities that I remember vividly was that she used to possess an unconditional friendly attitude, establishing distinctions with whoever she was greeting.

Little did I realize, concerning this encounter at the ward, that perhaps it would be the last time I was going to see Linda alive, because just a few weeks later, I received depressing news that she had passed away while resting in bed, thus succumbing after coming out of remission for some time. There is no doubt that our Lord called her quite earlier than usual in order to spare her from further suffering, the tremendous sacrifice ordeal that she had to endure during the last part of the year of her existence on Earth. One thing is obviously for sure, Linda will be in my mind for as long as I may live, so help me oh merciful Almighty God. In the meantime, while reflecting on Linda's life, let's not forget to mention that she was a significant part and the topic of conversation among all those who were very lucky to meet this very special person. Time will pass, but her memories will remain in our hearts for as long as we live.

While all of this sad development has taken place at the Hospital for the last past weeks, in the meantime, back home, my dear wife is already approaching her seventh month stage of pregnancy. Everybody in our families are becoming extremely excited, and the prayers to our Heavenly Father are becoming more than intensified.

I must emphasize, based on my personal observation, and it is certainly true, that Clemencia is really doing a fabulous job preparing for the day when she is due for delivery since time is becoming closer for the baby's arrival. She is keeping herself physically and psychologically fit by expressing a great deal of confident awareness to what is forthcoming ahead, exercising consistently under a rigorous plan, as well as following a strict supervised diet to ensure the unborn baby is properly receiving adequate nutrients, therefore, assuring a safe journey into his or her ultimate destination, life on planet Earth, a very complex place beyond reasonable doubt. A drastic change from a simple sedentary interior lifestyle is soon to end. No comparison to the nasty hostility in the exterior environment that there is to offer, certainly not his or her preferable selection, that is a clear fact as it may be. Anticipation is gaining formidable momentum as to what will be upon masterfully displaying a grandeur arrival, culminating with a traditional tearfully emotional grand finale.

Chapter 16

On a previous visit to the Hospital, I was directly approached by the doctor with "great news", and I quote her saying it very clearly. She also said, "once again it is time for you, Mr. William, to be ready for another intravenous procedure", thus a scheduled appointment has been officially requested within the next couple of weeks. It will be a second intravenous medication dosage, which along with the extreme toxic drug chemical component, has become undoubtedly a nemesis to a great majority of patients like me who already have been exposed to it, obviously with very negative results and reactions ever since the time we all had taken it, starting from day one. Anticipating what is coming ahead, I am starting to feel very uncomfortable, kind of nervous, exactly after listening to the doctor's latest order. This second intravenous procedure is complying with a projected research program protocol that has been officially set, thus, following an alternated calendar sequence for special strong medication.

Why in particular is this one situation so critical? Very well! There exists a remote possibility concerning the time scheduled, which creates a conflict of interest more probably during the time when I may be admitted to the Hospital for such a reason already previously mentioned. I am referring to the severe symptoms caused by strong side effects from such peculiar toxic medication once it is injected into the body, then, another possibility lays on

Clemencia's natural ability for delivering the baby accordingly to the calculated projection date, perhaps, it may be pure coincidence if they occur on exactly the same date, simultaneously indeed. I am a little bit nervous, but hopefully praying that God willing, with perfect timing, end results will turn favorable in everybody's best interest.

It turned out to be perfect timing since I underwent the cycle procedure according to the official schedule. I was physically uncomfortable for a couple of days, however, as time passed by, I was able to return to work in full force, then, about two weeks later, family history was made when Clemencia, after several agonizing hours, finally delivered our beautiful baby girl, a bundle of love who was born absent from complications, thanks to the Lord, Alleluia.

As expected, considering the circumstances involved, Ingrid has been bestowed with special distinction, thus, becoming the first baby to be born amongst our siblings, God's precious blessing gift. Destiny had it that Clemencia and I had been chosen among the two families, fourteen brothers and sisters, for this historical and memorable event, the first grandchild for our parents' delight.

In spite of a jubilee spirit, some sort of disagreement arose between family members, basically precipitating unto a temporary minor chaos, created precisely because of the different opinions concerning our baby's official name "Ingrid Clemencia", which became our final unanimous decision, irrevocable, to say the least. They all naturally wanted us to follow the traditional custom of selecting her name after Clemencia's grandmothers or any other closer relative for that matter. However, we were determined to break away from traditions, and my dear wife stood behind me. I did turn around, and in appreciation to her loyalty, Ingrid's middle name Clemencia was introduced, for everybody's delight. I succeeded by breaking away from the old traditions, iact est fabula.

Recapitulating my experience of being subjected just recently for the second time around to another intravenous medication, the toxic drug symptom reaction turned out not to be any worse than previously administered back in Autumn of last year, when, for the first time I was subjected to such pitiful discomfort, strong convulsions, followed by a reaction of uncontrollable nausea, endless hours then to say the least, yes indeed.

Anyway, in conclusion I must mention how lucky I am, if considering that I had a prompt recovery afterward. And to my delight, I had more than sufficient time to prepare myself physically in order to partake in such a jubilee's moment of assisting Clemencia with the baby's crucial delivery stage. After almost nine months of tireless effort, ever since conception had taken place, and finally now, culminating the zenith of love in life's precious creation, we had immense gratitude to God for granting us such a majestic emotional historical moment in our lives: Rejoice! Yes, indeed because after my full recovery, Ingrecita was born exactly a week and a half later during a typical gorgeous sunny Spring day on Saturday, April 10th, 1965 at precisely 6:56 p.m., a date that shall be registered in the annals of my life somewhere deep in my heart for as long as I am destined to live.

Something important that I find quite undoubtedly worth mentioning is that back then in those days, we spouses were not allowed under any circumstance to be actually present in the final labor stage. Therefore, it was obviously, and extremely sad accepting the fact, with a great deal of regret, that I was not allowed to either participate nor to express any type of moral support and physical comfort to my beloved wife. I do clearly remember though being seated in the waiting room waiting for any news or announcement quite impatiently, when all of sudden, one of the nurses on duty approached me to ask me to pick up the telephone in order to listen to the doctor's latest report on our new baby, and of course Clemencia's general physical condition after almost 16 hours since she was admitted into Saint John General Hospital at Elmhurst, Queens, New York.

Immediately after, the entire anticipated announcement was made to all relatives, friends, and acquaintances. The inevitable moment of truth would be coming soon, closer than I expected, for me to inform the doctors and medical staff of the secret that I had concealed for over nine months. There was not a basic explanation as to why they were not informed concerning Clemencia's pregnancy status; undoubtedly, it was a serious mistake on my part, perhaps, ignorance as time did prove to be right. That is exactly my sole answer and this haunted my mind for years to come.

Upon arriving at the Clinic for a regular appointment, about a week later after Ingrecita was born, I walked into the Center with a great deal of determination, and a firm resolution to focus on announcing to the doctors the wonderful news concerning my family's additional member. They had certainly been in suspense. Listening for a while to what I had to say, the scenario obviously eventually turned chaotic immediately upon following my disclosure. Their natural reaction became imminent, a typical attitude of shock, then turning around to expressing seriousness, their faces almost in disbelief, to say the least. What ensued next was a series of advice, a sort of confrontation toward my persona's ineffectiveness by not taking any initiative toward informing them about our family's future expansion back when conception occurred. They went ahead to illustrate and make me aware of the serious perilous consequences that might have resulted and affected the embryo. And of course, Clemencia's life/health threatening condition as well! They convincingly acknowledged their conclusion based on past history records and incidents involving other patients with related cases. Evidently, their concern was perfectly correct; there was not a doubt considering the fact that I had been exposed to a variety of toxic related drugs while indefinitely undergoing an experimental chemotherapy treatment.

Doctors Clarkson and Gilbert, quite fully recovered after regaining their composure from such a state of shock, or should I better say «nightmare", did not waste any time in imparting their recommendations should this occur again. What ensued next was a series of medical explanations illustrating to me that I should not hesitate a day, or a week, to comply with the Doctor's recommendations to please immediately bring it to their attention in order for them to take the proper professional approach, thus, assuring a safe supervision during Clemencia's second pregnancy period, if that would be the case. Having said that, this incident would haunt me for the rest of my life, oh yes, indeed.

Two months have already passed by since Clemencia was discharged from the hospital after delivering a new baby member to our family. It is hard to realize how time flies or rather said, flies fast up and away just like an airplane. Having said that, it is almost impossible to accept such a simple life reality. In the meantime, we are having such a wonderful experience caring for our precious infant daughter. Somehow, we get the impression that in spite of her natural tender limitations, she is already starting to develop some awareness of the world surrounding her and showing excellent signs of improved reflexes within her limited confinement. I recall seeing her jump up and down in her crib imitating what she saw on the television. Our joy is compounded with homage and humble gratitude towards the Lord for bestowing upon us such a precious creature, a tiny bundle of love. Having said that, we reach our conclusion that there is not a greater moment in life's personal experiences than giving birth, procreating, yes, quite indeed.

Chapter 17

The month of June is just around the corner and very soon another summer season will be upon us again. Hopefully, we should be blessed with a dry pleasant weather, let's see if that will be the case indeed. In the meantime, as I am walking into the Outpatient Clinic, I receive the sad news that a couple of patients who I had met since the first time when I was being admitted to the Hospital, dating back to March of last year (1964), had passed away. They had succumbed to the disease complications, or perhaps related to a combination of factors like stressful inside effects resulting from toxic drugs, or part of the demanding experimental research program.

One patient, in particular, whom I will refer to as "Thomas" because I can't recall his name, was a former Sunken Meadow High School teacher who at the time I first met him, was already going through Chemotherapy treatment. He was married to a very distinguished lady and they had a young adolescent boy who I used to see sporadically whenever he was off from school, also quite distinguished and a well behaved kid. My correct guess is that I shall not be seeing both of them again anymore.

The reason why I especially remember Thomas is due to an incident that occurred one day while we were seated, talking with some of the other patients, when all of a sudden while checking his arm he started to curse the blood running through his veins, obviously responsible for his ailment. Although it was something quite spontaneous, probably unintentional and perhaps out of despair, it was his immediate response upon realizing his serious mistake of imposing strong language remarks, to turn around excusing himself for verbally expressing himself with such an audacious attitude and tone of voice. Meanwhile, his face still revealed a crystal clear expression of sadness and sorrow.

I reflected back on my mother's intuition related to mortality. My mother was perfectly correct and very confident while being engaged in any educational conversation. Especially when we all were seated around the dining table, she would become the chief in command and we would not have any other choice but to remain calm and ask common sense questions while listening to her well calculated answers, highly rich in wisdom. It has been such a long time as I try to recall those days when we first started to comprehend, learning from her own personal experience. She used to mention to us that in spite of the fact that she never continued education after her high school graduation, she was extremely disciplined, and usually opted for reading a minimum of seven illustrative books annually. Besides, her experience traveling, and living in far distance lands, became basically the major contributor that enriched her source of intellectual knowledge. If the topic was related specifically to immortality, obviously, it would bring curiosity to a high level with responses to "what was there beyond death?" anecdotes. She would come forward with diverse illustrations that we would find quite interesting or sometimes rather uneasy to comprehend. Having said that, she would constantly mention and remind us that life on Planet Earth was typically subject to Mother Nature's multiple limitations, more specifically, to a brief existence, or the equivalent of a profound dream. These were some of the numerous approaches taken, constantly reminding us about our simple mortality origin.

Chapter 18

A few months after Clemencia's full recovery from her postpartum, we were highly advised on a few occasions by the doctors' eminent professional recommendation, that it would be a wise decision to immediately consider a basic harmless family planning program, involving safe approaches to birth prevention. Undoubtedly, this was a significant major responsible decision to ensue next in this day and time, also considering the physical status I was seriously suffering, while undergoing an experimental cancer research chemotherapy program. Therefore, if we were to practice the traditional rhythm or any other alternatives available at present time, there was no doubt about the odds against preventing pregnancy that were highly risky, based on medical statistic reports.

Sooner than expected, we opted to consider calling the Hospital to make an appointment and set arrangements with a social worker who would help us select the most appropriate decision concerning a safety device system for pregnancy prevention. Once we finally met with a young female representative, and after proper introduction was made, she went ahead and started illustrating to us the various advantages and disadvantages, which carry not only physical but psychological effects, as well. She emphasized how some safety devices would affect Clemencia's future if she reconsidered becoming pregnant again, later on, as time was concerned.

Once our private consultation with the social worker was finally concluded, the next agenda was evidently to call immediately to set an appointment with the doctors for a private consultation concerning our family's future status. Therefore, it would be imperative for us to listen to their professional advice and be ready to prepare to follow whatever recommendations would be more logically appropriate according to the seriousness of the situation involved. What would ensue next? Perhaps, they would search for some of the latest innovative clinical safety devices, conditionally selected as a prevention alternative for unique cases where pregnancy is endangering. It is introduced for our approval, of course, providing that we should not contemplate any remote possibility, and relinquishing any sentimental intention, of considering a future addition to the family.

So much moral calculated value was a factor to be considered, as far as future planned parenthood was concerned; besides, let's not ignore my life expectancy. While still uncertain, ever since I was struck with this terminal disease, how miraculous it has been for me to be able to stay in remission for over a year. The Lord has been very generous to me, and so far His divine goodness has spared my life. Having said that, with inspiration during times of solitude and profound reflection, I have reached a paramount conclusion, believing the Lord has chosen me to carry a very important special mission on Earth. I am only a humble servant, but it is the greatest honor for me even though I am not worth of His mercy. Yet, in order to fulfill my assignment with profound determination, an emissary I shall be until the coming of judgment day, so help me God.

After very deep soul searching, we finally have reached a serious conclusion, and that is, the sooner the better. That was our ultimate determination. Obviously, there was not any other alternative to contemplate considering that we were running out of time selecting an adequate family plan method where a contraceptive device is concerned. Alas! Anticipating that my next outpatient clinic visit date was approaching, we opted to directly call the doctor's secretary to make an appointment for Clemencia's visit. If feasible, we wanted to schedule her appointment exactly the same day, but immediately preceding my regular outpatient visit. Because of a conflict in scheduling, we were able to get Clemencia's appointment on the same day, but right after my outpatient visit.

Upon concluding my regular visit, we were instructed to walk straight ahead to the nurses' station, where they should more than gladly provide us with the directions to the doctor's office location. They instructed us that the location happened to be exactly a short walking distance across from 68th Street North into the adjacent building where evidently Doctor Clarkson, and his colleagues, were already waiting for orientation, thus, preparing us to be familiar with some of the most preferable safe approach methods pertaining to pregnancy prevention. Clemencia and I had already reached an irreversible decision, needless to mention, perhaps a choice that was not one that we wanted to make, but that was in our best personal interest considering the odds we were against. Undoubtedly, there was no other alternative to contemplate but true life reality, certainly indeed. It was really an extremely difficult path to follow.

Great Scott! After witnessing a team discussion, a decision was unanimously accepted, definitely selecting perhaps what would become the most adequate safe medical approach as far as pregnancy prevention was concerned. Once the meeting came to conclusion, Doctor Alfred Gilbert decided to explain in Spanish, our native language, for better clarification purposes, a thorough detailed illustration of how the entire surgical procedure would be performed. It would be accomplished under maximum safety regulations, and with minimum discomfort for the patient during the entire surgical procedure. He even went further, giving us details on how the surgery would be performed, and I quote saying: "in the uterus formandoce uterine bebe fallopian tubes."

Upon terminating the medical meeting, and expressing our most profound gratitude to Doctor Gilbert for taking precious time of his own in order to avoid any doubts or unnecessary questions preceding the long overdue surgery soon to take place. He was just concerned and wanted to make sure that every single recommendation was perfectly understood that transpired during the doctors' meeting, thus avoiding any personal conflict of interest.

Once the meeting reached its conclusion, we hastily left the doctor's office precisely which ended up being during the rush hour; apparently, we had no choice but to follow the flow. Before it could be prevented, all of a sudden, we joined the masses of people disappearing into early evening hours, I am quite doubtless they were destined mostly to home sweet home.

"That our day will come" was exactly what was in our minds, obviously wondering how many days we may have to wait, expecting a telephone call from the Memorial Hospital doctor's office with official confirmation pertaining to Clemencia's forthcoming surgery. Therefore, since we were in such a state of suspense anticipating the notification call, we opted to distract ourselves by starting to make adequate arrangements for Clemencia's last minute personal details. Days passed and we finally received a call from the doctor's secretary Bonnie, informing us that everything had been officially set for surgery and that it would be appropriate for her to come earlier in order to become familiar with pre-surgery technical guidelines.

Anticipating a very busy day ahead, I immediately decided to call my mother to make a special request, asking her to keep

Clemencia in her prayers and to provide moreal support. Mother wisely replied to "leave everything in the Lord's divine hands." She also took the opportunity to remind me of the importance of keeping one's strong faith, even in times of despair. Our brief conversation was marred with a touch of emotional feelings, of course, and sending to Clemencia best wishes, and warmest regards.

Somewhere around early afternoon, we walked out of the house hastily, trying to avoid the typical commuting inconvenience during the rush hours for which the major urban cosmopolitan cities are notoriously known. The city of New York absolutely is not an exception by all standards. We did quite well as far as commuting into the city; we really felt an aura of greatness as if we had accomplished something extraordinary by establishing an amazing new traveling record time worthy of the Guinness Book of Records, yes indeed.

We finally expressed relief once we entered the Hospital main entrance. A few minutes later we were being welcomed by staff nurses who already had my wife's chart ready for the doctor's last minute review. Obviously they were anxiously waiting to guide us across York Avenue towards New York Hospital where surgery would be immediately performed. It was close to 4:30 P.M. when we finally were introduced to the doctor who would be in charge of the surgery proceedings. What ensued next? Well, a few minutes later after emotional feelings were displayed and farewell concluded, Clemencia was led by a nurse straight to the Surgical ward located nearby. In the meantime, I did stay behind by the visitors' comfort area, while my wife disappeared from sight as she was directed away.

Two hours passed and there was no communication, neither from the Doctor, nor his assistants, concerning the surgery outcome. I obviously started experiencing concern as to why surgery was taking so long. Alas, no sooner was I starting to become in a ferociously entangled state of mind, when suddenly, I saw my wife coming seated in a wheelchair led by a nurse who was holding some envelopes in her uniform pocket. Clemencia was looking normal, in spite of the fact she just had undergone surgery, remarkable! The nurse provided the envelopes specifically describing information that Clemencia would have to follow during the critical post-recovery period, as well as medical prescriptions in case any discomfort or pain would arise.

Clemencia was instructed to rest and lie down on the visitor's couch for a minimum of an hour. In the meantime, I called Roberto's home to let him know that we should be ready within an hour, thus allowing him sufficient time to drive back to New York Hospital precisely during the late evening chaotic traffic. By this time, I said to myself "why not kill two birds with one stone?" Therefore, I decided to stop by the Hospital's Apothecary, and fill the doctor's prescription with the Pharmacist. Well, as we were waiting to pick up the medication, all of sudden Roberto arrived stepping into the visitor's reception area. What a relief it really was seeing him arrive so soon, considering the late afternoon congested traffic indeed.

As soon as Clemencia officially was discharged, a few minutes later we found ourselves walking directly to the main hospital exit, and straight to the visitors' parking area. Immediately after taking access into the automobile, Roberto drove looking for the nearest parking exit. Once out, he made a left turn on York Avenue going south to the Queensboro Bridge entrance located by 59th Street, and then straight across to the Borough of Queens, the typical route connecting two Boroughs, Queens and Manhattan. This coincidentally became a familiar route that I followed after M.S.K Hospital became my second designated residence.

As soon as we started crossing the bridge we could not resist turning around, contemplating such an impressive view, practically irresistible while overlooking Manhattan's spectacular late evening scenario, disappearing from sight as Roberto drove speeding away. That said, in a santiamen we finally arrived in Queens. By then I could not help notice Roberto's uneasy curiosity, initiating some conversation, trying to find out how this day's agenda transpired, particularly during Clemencia's surgery. It really did not take me long to disclose to him a complete account of precisely how everything was accomplished during the day's events, while in the meantime, I was imploring the Lord for his divine interception on Clemencia's behalf, Amen.

As we were almost reaching final destination, we realized how a "little bit" late it was by now, perhaps close to 9:30 P.M. We requested that Roberto join us for a light dinner in one of our neighborhood restaurants. Needless to mention he declined our invitation, expressing some consideration for Clemencia, however we both persistently insisted, and succeeded twisting his elbow. Ha! Ha!

Life is a Dream Part 2

As time is passing, life really has become less stressful now-a-days, obviously judging from my personal perception. It is attributed to a recent turn of events taking place, encouraging indeed, which was a combination of undergoing a new protocol schedule which was selected by my doctor's revised experimental procedures concerning my prolonged treatment, as well as my strong Spiritual values. The Lord generously has bestowed blessings upon my soul during these critical years of endless battle for ultimate survival against Cancer. Thus prostrated in front of Your Divine presence, I profoundly offer homage, thanksgiving for all favors bestowed upon Your humble servant, as I really am a pilgrim of this World, Amen!

Now with the latest development in the medical series, I shall start going for clinical appointments every other week. Needless to say, I am so delighted, and why not may I say? Well! I really am very optimistic anticipating life's brighter future outlook, it is bringing relief anticipating that no further symptoms might reappear again or stage out of remission, God willing. And it definitely will create more flexible time, undoubtedly the ideal scenario. Realizing that from now on, I shall have more ample time available especially concerning personal affairs, and considering that from this moment on, obviously I shall be working additional days in my job occupation. As far as financial concerns, this will reflect personal income gains.

Something worth mention concerns my self-imposed double standard, which I progressively have confronted during the last five years. The simple fact is that I have been holding jobs, and simultaneously undergoing a rigorous complicated treatment, with great expectation that some miracle may occur concerning this terminal disease afflicting my health. Therefore after deep soul searching, I cleverly opted to keep my health issues, the simple fact that I am actively enrolled in a voluntary Chemo treatment program, under the strictest secrecy possible. Thus I must be extra careful at work, really restraining myself from divulging true issues, otherwise running a high risk that my job might be terminated. That said, I believed that I was acting within acceptable guidelines, acting cautiously for my own sake, keeping this secret contained. Had I seriously considered mentioning to my superiors my medical history case, a terminal disease in which I was still undergoing treatment and consistently in a stage of remission, if I had opted for a transparency approach, they probably would have contemplated the health issue and seriously rejected the idea of hiring me because of the latest statistical data. According to recent medical data reports published, there was absolutely no chance, or a remote possibility, for a cancer patient's survival anywhere on earth's six continents.

It really is unbelievable that throughout these years I have managed to hold jobs uninterrupted wherever I worked. My superiors always were flexible concerning my work schedule for any of my fictitious versions of why I needed some dispensation in taking time off. I definitely was treated with exceptional consideration, allowing me to take days off depending on clinical follow ups already stipulated. Undoubtedly, I have been blessed by my Lord Heavenly Father, Amen!

I hereby am describing in full details my real personal experience taking toxic medication since the treatment commenced five years ago. It really is remarkable how during this time period, my body's immunity to a certain drug gradually started showing major improvement as time passed. In spite of the fact that I really was unable to develop any type of immunity system per se to the chemical agents, I was able to control devastating reactions typically associated with chemo components. Of course, slowly but surely significant progress has been accomplished! For instance, a typical illustration is how the digestive system now is assimilating foods by holding them further than previously registered. That said, the exact average number of hours related to gastric reaction to toxic medication was approximately 3 hours before viciously experiencing side effects. Obvious it was common during the first 3 year period. The next year reached an average between 4 to 5 hours. Starting from the fifth year on, I firmly was able to control the fatidic reaction for longer time periods, perhaps a little closer to 6 hours before physically succumbing to the terrifying convulsions. Without employing exaggeration, I just felt like dying, to say the least. From my personal observation, I really have reached the conclusion that faith, determination, and perseverance undoubtedly have been primary factors for partial recovery. I presently experience discomfort as if I'm entangled on a royal titanic battle against this deadly disease best defined as Leukemia, Cancer of the blood. So help me Lord.

A historical sequence of events have taken place through this year 1968, particularly during the month of August when I finally submitted my application request for naturalization documents to the Immigration Department by filling a petition to embrace United States of America citizenship, thus relinquishing my Colombian national status. Once again my brother Roberto came forward! He did volunteer to become one of my two required witnesses, also Mrs. Celia Mercado, a very pleasant lady, senior citizen, and neighbor of ours originally from the city of San Juan, Puerto Rico. Of course both were United States citizens. What a memorable occasion I did experience once we walked into the Federal Immigration Center. That date when I finally took the pledge of allegiance to my newly adopted country in a formal ceremonious ambience, well! As far back as my thoughts can recollect, never before in my life had I really been surrounded by such a conglomeration of citizens from diverse nationalities, races, and creeds. There reigned emotional euphoria under such a solemn atmosphere. It really was an indescribable moment, a profoundly spiritual feeling, an over-

joyful ambience within the Center once the ceremony was concluded. Everybody officially had been bestowed with great honor, and received their citizenship documentation as well; consequently, we have become citizens of this vast wonderland, which we proudly call the United States of America. It really is a great privilege, and highly honorable, embracing my new heritage.

Something extremely important I have failed to mention all these years is the simple fact that during this perilous time, besides holding a job and taking care of family financial obligations, that with Clemencia's tremendous support I was able to continue my education by attending technical school after work, studying with full determination pursuing an equivalent Associates Degree in Construction Technology. That said, precisely this year in 1968 was my graduation ceremony following 4 intensive years registered in the Technical School evening sessions; therefore it was a perfect time for celebration, undoubtedly my personal opinion is that it obviously was long overdue. Nonetheless, I am very grateful to the Lord for allowing me to culminate the zenith of one of my dreams I have had, during these unpredictable times. Undoubtedly a gigantic goal achievement, yes indeed.

What ensued next? Upon finishing my education I immediately started to reconsider switching from my present occupation, seeking a new job in the field related to my recent acquired degree. Needless to mention, from the beginning it was not that easy, but rather complicated. Let me elaborate on my statement; sometimes searching for a job turned very frustrating, especially while searching with a great deal of tenacity for open positions. In reality it took several months of knocking on doors, filling out applications, and delivering resumes before, alas!, I finally was granted an interview, and almost instantly became a candidate for the open position, thus with a guarantee for a permanent position - if I was hired, of course! The Company name was American Insurance Association, headquartered at Williamsburg Bank edifice located by Nassau and Williams Streets, about 4 blocks west of Broadway Avenue, in the downtown Manhattan zone better known as the Manhattan Canyon because of the sky riser buildings, and the dark narrow streets, a short distance to the World Trade Center. After I was hired, as time passed, I miraculously adapted myself quite well, more or less, and henceforth became accustomed to work's new schedule, as well as the rigorous urban commuting.

One day while returning home from work, a profound mystical idea struck my mind. Thus ip-so-facto, I reached the conclusion that perhaps it would be perfect timing to commit myself and my family to a pilgrimage, attending Sunday's holy mass service in the city for a period of ten consecutive weeks, to offer Thanksgiving and pay Homage to one of the most beloved Catholic Saints, and obtaining from our Almighty Heavenly Father all spiritual blessings. I am referring to Saint Anthony, patron of the most desperate cases assisting with powerful intercession. He has been my favorite Saint ever since I can recall, going back to adolescent years. Consequently, after consulting with my dear wife regarding my spiritual Damascus revelation, we decided to start a pilgrimage to Saint Francis Assisi›s National Catholic Shrine located right on 31ˢᵗ Street, between Broadway and 7ᵗʰ avenue, adjacent to Gimbels department store in midtown Manhattan. Why there, so far from home? Well! The simple reason for selecting this sanctuary was because it has been my mother's favorite Church for prayer and spiritual meditation for years. It is a majestic edifice in the center of such a mundane atmosphere, it is quite close to her job location; and it is the invidious location of Saint Anthony's imposing statue. As far as commuting concerns, accessibility is just perfectly convenient to reach from any corner location within the metropolitan area. Alea est iact! This was the immortal statement pronounced by great Roman General Emperor Julius Caesar, translated to "the die is cast," meaning "no going back," rather forward once decision is ultimately taken.

Prior to our forthcoming religious pilgrimage to Saint Francis National Shrine, we bowed our heads humbly imploring The Lord to bestow upon us His blessing, and granting strength and determination to accomplish our endeavor. So much was there at stake contemplating our typical religious missionary task; getting up early Sunday mornings sometimes could be discouraging enough just at the thought of traveling to Manhattan. If it did not represent sacrifice enough, then let's not forget winter's extremely blistering cold temperature, which coincidentally was rapidly approaching upon us without any sign of major relief. Obviously, this vicious temperature could be another discouraging factor indeed, from fulfilling our missionary plans; however only firm determination would play such an important role, offsetting some unpredictable hurdles that might develop during the season, keeping our faith in high stem. The personal end result would be profound moral satisfaction, to say the least.

Once our 10 visit schedule to Saint Anthony was set, we opted selecting the first Sunday in October to start attending regular

Mass service at Saint Francis National Shrine. We really became engulfed with such profound jubilee as time finally approached, ready to begin our sacred pilgrim to the Sanctuary. Beforehand, we came up with a brilliant idea. Thus we definitely agreed, why not kill 2 birds with one stone, realizing that since we would be going to the city for our spiritual commitment, we strongly considered for our personal mutual satisfaction and recreation that it would be terrific staying around town the rest of the day enjoying some major attractions the city has so much to offer. Therefore, we decided to incorporate it by simply staying over as planned. How advantageous would it be for our lovely Ingrid to receive a little bit of exposure to such an enchanted city life scenario? Undoubtedly, as time passed, Manhattan's Central Park became Ingrid's favor attraction. We religiously contemplated turning her favorite recreational city site into another pilgrimage, as well. Needless to mention, what a wonderful experience we had that first day, and ever since.

It is hard to believe that in this year 1968 only a few months still remain in the calendar in anticipation of the forthcoming annual winter holidays. During this year, my greatest satisfactions have been a paramount success; great end results culminated in accomplishments successfully obtained as the year approaches its end. As for relinquishing my nationality, I officially have become citizen of United States of America, precisely 9 years after immigrating to this wonderful land. Followed by thoroughly completing my education, slowly but surely, escalating my personal status. Meanwhile, upon graduation, I was able to acquire a highly technical position. Culminating in the most important encouraging news concerning the Chemo treatment program, the latest reports indicating positive results, of course!

I was highly cautious in developing expectations since 4 years ago when I was registered in the Chemo research program. All this time I really have been blessed, staying for such a long time period in a stage of remission, free from major side effects, with only a few exceptions as far I can recall; one being the strong toxic medication taken every other month of which any patient hardly has been able to tolerate the magnitude of its chemical component. Also, unexpected side effects I occasionally am susceptible to going through, the agonizing experience of feeling nauseated, continuing with some high degree of discomfort, and followed by a sort of pain in any part of my anatomy. It was unpredictable when it would strike or how lasting the time period might be. However I try not to become panicked, on the contrary, I just simply ignore it, pretending for it to be an isolated case associated with common side effects related to the treatment's tenacious result. Nonetheless, all these years I have reached the conclusion that unless the pain continuously perseveres, thus turning into a serious life threatening condition, only then would it be imperative reporting it to the doctor's personal attention. That said, I honestly believe there are times in one's life when keeping silent pertaining to your health reflexes might be acceptable, even if life is in peril.

The winter season finally arrived displaying its triumphal return, blistering winds, excruciatingly cold weather, and let's not forget such massive snow storms typically associated with the season. Once again this is just another indicative sign that we already are approaching another year end faster than expected. Holiday's solemn music sound, encompassed with festivity celebration, shall be upon all of us people of good will, from all corners of the Globe. This sign of the time undoubtedly will set you in the holiday's spirit making you realize that the greatest holiday of all is just upon us. What a wonderful time of the year is forthcoming, anticipating so much preparation for the once a year special holiday celebration and contagious jubilee reigning spirit, brotherly camaraderie among peoples of diversified faith, becoming contagious to the spiritual reflection, joy, and devotion, which undoubtedly is the order of the day. Chanukah, Christmas, and New Year holidays coincidentally are annually celebrated universally like no other festivities in the anal of human race history.

What wonderful memories I am carrying to my tomb. Well! After deep soul searching I have reached the conclusion that Christmas, Hanukah, and New Year's holiday celebrations, the first time spent in the city, has been nothing short of a sensational experience. Day after day while commuting to work, I have had great opportunities to attend some Holiday classical music concerts appropriated for the occasion which were held at Chase Manhattan Bank Park Plaza, downtown Manhattan's busiest district, a conglomerate of religious, financial, and government centers. Amazing! That is my impression of how the buildings' façades artistically have been decorated with multiple colorful holiday motive displays. Goodwill ambiance, and a collective aura of peace on Earth, is reigning among us creatures. It's overtones are really so classic; the religious symbolic significance reminding people from all Christian faiths of the primary reason of the celebration commemorating the birth anniversary of the greatest King that has ever lived, Our Lord Jesus Christ. What a terrific time we definitely have enjoyed during this holiday season in the city, simultaneously attending our traditional Sunday's pilgrimage to Saint Francis Shrine, and staying over after concluding our spiritual obligation. We would treat ourselves to a succulent breakfast, followed by taking a stroll or public transportation, whatever alternative was more convenient depending upon the distance factor. There were numerous destinations to select; while visiting points of interest most main attractions were watching holiday's decoration displays. Our daughter soon will be turning 4 years old, therefore she is becoming more aware of her natural surroundings. Hence, for the first time in her short life existence, she really is so fascinated, enjoying whatever is taking place, particularly during the holiday season celebration.

Once holiday season's exuberant celebration is over, great memories deeply remain in my soul: wonderful parties, sharing emotional gift exchanges, memorable reunion with relatives and friends in a joyful atmosphere of spirit of brotherhood, visiting extraordinary places, office work parties, bosses, and workers together sincerely expressing holiday best wishes and good will. Let's not forget the traditional toast with champagne, wine, or beer culminating in the company party celebration. There is something quite interesting that I definitely could not help noticing, realizing this was that time of the year when unlimited liquors were the day's order, freely served and allowed for general consumption under management's discretionary consent - everywhere on our planet Earth! Ha! Ha!

I am already contemplating my personal forthcoming milestone event that will occur in the new year, of course, providing it is in Our Lord's divine plans. On March 22 of this year of 1969, a memorable date to reckon with, I shall be celebrating my fifth year anniversary since I first was admitted at Elmhurst Public General Hospital with a rare symptom maligned disease, a series of internal complications that six months later officially was diagnosed as Leukemia Lymphoma-tic type cancer of the blood after their Medical Research Specialist team underwent a complete exploration performance, therefore reaching conclusive results. More positive news is that I have been in a stage of remission ever since, except during the first 5 months while still in observation right after being admitted to the Hospital. Negative symptom signs have not yet indicated per se, any particular recurrence as of this date. Oh! Lord humbly prostrated on my knees, I do offer Thanksgiving to you, loving God, for your mercies bestowed upon my soul.

Beginning January 1969, precisely on my second visit to the outpatient clinic, following a little bit of social protocol, I formally introduced myself to a group of patients who just recently were admitted to the Cancer Lymphoma research program unit. Among some of them, I clearly remember quite well, becoming very much impressed with Mrs. Cynthia Puglia, a young lady in her early 30's whose personal attributes was any lady's "envious" desire. She happened to possess an attractive figure, a pleasant charming personality, and was stunningly gorgeous indeed. That said, well, with such high attributes it took not much longer before she became very popular among us, and medical staff as well! As time went on, we became very familiar with her previous medical history case, almost fatidic end results. It was similar to a familiar malpractice case involving private doctors reaching wrong controversial diagnoses, prescribing wrong medication, and automatically creating a more complicated critical stage, jeopardizing the patient's poorly existing health condition. Obviously, since having experienced similar controversial decisions, my best spiritual advice was encouraging her to keep a strong profound faith in God, the doctors, and herself. I told her that it has been a personal motto I have followed ever since being persistently entangled in such an unpredictable endless battle, a crusade mission to overcome this dreadful disease, medically defined as Leukemia, cancer of the blood. Therefore, on several occasions, Cynthia and I would be engaged in a conversation reminiscing about common personal experiences that we went through when first struck with cancer. Undoubtedly, I always emphasized that my strong spiritual convictions really have been primarily a shield throughout these long surviving years, thus an infallible path I have sought faithfully for partial recovery, day by day.

Among newly admitted patients there was a very distinguished middle aged professor, a west coast resident who would be commuting from Los Angeles, California to New York City once a month, staying in town a minimum of two full days, of course depending on his blood analysis laboratory results. My kudos goes to him for his displayed will power and self-determination in overcoming once and for all his fated illness, probably the most fierce battle ever taken in his entire life's existence. He will be supervised simultaneously at two prestigious clinical institutions, one in the state of California, and another in New York. I personally wish him the best there is to be, and to hopefully be able to endure the rigor that the treatment demands, as well as the stressful inconvenience during his long transcontinental flight. Hopefully the Lord will bestow blessings upon him while on his ultimate goal mission, seeking positive alternatives, leading to partial, perhaps complete recovery. Let's not forget that miracles can happen, anytime, anywhere, anyway; hopefully that will be his destiny.

A series of developments have taken place at the Outpatient Clinic, during the early part of this year, starting first with Doctor Clarkson's former private secretary Jessica, who I greatly had the pleasure of meeting five years ago. She never became engaged in any friendly conversation, or revealed forthcoming intentions of leaving her position and searching for new horizons; she really kept it under a most strict low profile. When the news broke out about quitting her job, it was a tremendous surprise for all of us who knew her for a long time; we obviously had not had the opportunity to express our best wishes to her future endowments. One thing definitely is certain I must say, she was friendly, always conducted herself with compassion and respect, special qualities to say the least. However, she was possessed with an introverted personality, a typical characteristic of hers.

Another development was on a personal level; after thoroughly reviewing my recovery progress history, a doctor's team has reached a unanimous decision which I have received with a great deal of satisfaction. Considering my medical history statute, my positive response to chemotherapy treatment, and my present state of mind, which I have been quite luckily enjoying all these years of my life, they really have given serious consideration to a major revision in my treatment plan. Therefore upon concluding intensive laboratory testing with positive results, they definitely have decided going forward to make whatever necessary protocol changes may be required. Since I consistently have been in a stage of remission, it obviously made me a special perfect candidate. One in particular is that I shall be coming for regular clinic follow-up appointments every other week, in lieu of once a week. In addition, the bone marrow specimens schedule generally will be performed once a month, providing that treatment is marching on the right course. There probably will be a few exceptions to the rule; this basically will depend on the doctor's criterion request. I categorically am bewildered with joy, obviously encouraging news indeed upon my medical stipulation's latest development.

What wonderful memories have occurred during my life's bygone years. Some of them represent a special recollection and display of emotional feelings resulting from my experiences. I have shared them with terrific fellow patients whose personal lives have been tragically afflicted one way or another by a cancer terminal disease. Unfortunately, we all are fully aware of our common eminent destiny in spite of the fact that of a remote possibility for survival, it is hardly existent. Obviously the odds for surviving is practically against us; but, somehow there still reigns in our hearts an extraordinary life revelation. We are hopefully looking for some sign of a miracle while still struggling with the great determination of an impossible dream. Obviously, I am referring to every day's perennial strife to survive, of course! We all are aware of the Lord's fundamental principle of creation, thus we shall be born to live and later to die; human nature in order of evolution which nobody, but nobody, will be able to be spared from such a celestial mandate.

I started reminiscing, going far back to the year 1964, the beginning of my life's long journey which happened when I officially became admitted at M.S.K. Hospital. I took a very deep soul search, recollecting a series of events that took place since then until present day. I definitely can say with a great deal of certainty that the number of patients who I personally have had the pleasure of meeting and sharing mutual common experiences were unforgettable moments. The fraternal atmosphere revealing our personal private lives, and now to realize that almost all of them have become statistical figures. They are no longer part of this living world of which very few among us still continue surviving in the stage of remission. Our Lord has taken them away to an eternal life in paradise. For their own sake, relief finally has touched them indeed. From my personal reflection they have been spared from their hopeless misery and constant suffering as well, thus bringing a great deal of relief; that is my spiritual conclusion.

This typical scenario was the rule. On any particular occasion, if I coincidentally was engaged in a pleasant conversation with a patient whose corporal appearance apparently seemed to be doing very well for that matter, it really wasn't the case. As time passed their conditions would end up with the same results. Either the patient would have passed away by succumbing to the cancer itself, or strong toxic medications had been administered which ironically turned out to be as fatal for some who were unable to tolerate the chemo components applied to counter attack the disease itself.

I always said again and again, that throughout these years, I have met thousands of patients who have walked through the Center and yet after enjoying the excellent camaraderie most of them are not around anymore. This is a sad and a touching situation. But somehow I have been able to overcome any sign of depression, sadness, or fear because I find losing someone who in a way also became a temporary part of one's life leaves behind a treasure of memories, before succumbing to an eminent death. Definitely this ominous scenario being described really is a typical example. It touches reality, therefore it might even have consequences of having positive psychological results. Its effect upon anyone whose personally underwent these conditions seems to possess a very strong attitude towards life's adversities, indeed.

Among the hundreds of patients who I have met throughout these years, there is one in particular I came to admire the most for a very special reason. Steve Goodman was his name, a resident from the city of Chicago, State of Illinois. His professional career background was an accomplished musician, who was better known among United States folk music circles. He really was an accomplished composer gifted with magnificent talent, quite versatile on writing his music, and lyrics. His unforgettable song "City of New Orleans" catapulted him into stardom. He really was very proud of collaborating with world renowned composer/performer Mr. Peter Siegel, and his select music group. On several occasions, when he would come to Outpatient Clinic's regular follow up visits, he would delight those of us lucky to be present by playing some of his songs with his favorite guitar companion. Unfortunately, the rigor of his professional performing schedule always kept him constantly under stressful conditions; the rest is pure history. Sometime during the decade of the late 70's, he sadly did succumb to the disease, leaving behind for posterity a musical legacy. Undoubtedly, he was the epitome of success. He will be in my treasured memories as long I might be destined to live, Amen!

What a wonderful experience I went through at the Outpatient Clinic on one particular occasion, while I was waiting to be called next for my follow up appointment. It precisely happened then as I was sitting quite comfortably relaxing, when all of sudden I was approached by Doctor Clarkson's secretary, Bonnie, who was conveying an important Doctor's message and I paraphrase: The Doctors periodically conduct presentations, a series of systematic lectures to Cornell Medical College student's faculty. Therefore they carefully are selecting some of the patients, whose long history of being in a stage of remission since afflicted by cancer disease make us perfect candidates for this endeavor, thus they presently are seeking volunteers.

Undoubtedly, after reaching conclusion of the message, my response was positive in santiamen. So much they have done for me all these years, and if I can contribute with some of my time, why not? That exactly was my rationale. Well! A couple of weeks later, those of us who were selected for this agenda directly received phone calls from doctor's office secretary Bonnie, giving instruction on the appointed date and time. It took not long before the day finally arrived for all of us to get together for the meeting. We were treated with a surprisingly joyful welcome, a token of appreciation for taking our personal time, and joining Doctors Bayard Clarkson and Alfred Gilvert for this special event. Apropos, soon they will be conducting a faculty lecture, but not without first having a preview presentation. It turned to be an experience of a lifetime, listening to these two luminary, eminent doctors addressing those who were there congregated, future prospective doctors attending the lecture. Of course, we patients who volunteered to participate in the lecture, briefly were requested to acknowledge the medical students there in attendance. A few questions we successfully anticipated with a great deal of serenity, indeed. Wow! What an unforgettable accumulation of memories, I really shall take with me to the grave. Oh! Lord accept my thanksgiving offers of your humble servant, Amen.

During the first months of 1969 the time came when I was due for another dose of a horrific toxic medication. After this procedure was done with an intravenous injection a brilliant idea came to my mind. Alas! I decided without hesitation to go straight to work rather than following the old traditional rush commuting to home to lay down and rest, thus impatiently waiting to confront what I typically have described through the years as my "Waterloo" encounter indeed. But before beginning my audacious journey to work, which took about 25 minutes, I stopped first by the Church located across the Hospital. I offered my thanksgiving, and pleading to strengthen my will. Oh! Lord. Realizing this was the first time since four years ago when I started taking these doses of toxic medication, my audacious decision was set, and perhaps would carry unpredictable repercussions; hopefully that would not be the case. I seriously admit, it was a critical decision considering the statute of limitation time involved. I kept on thinking I was going to be able to go home after work just on time before the devastating side effects would develop. That said, my anatomy tremors, anticipating a ferocious battle royal.

Once at work my coworkers and supervisor Paul Lefkowitz were surprised to see me there. Paul questioned me if everything was alright, since I never came to work the days I would take off for personal matters. My supervisor was delighted to see me, however he was very curious as to why I decided to come to work this day. I explained to him that my Doctor's follow up appointment was postponed last minute precisely while I still was traveling on my way to his office, therefore I did not hesitate a bit in taking a firm decision to come straight to work, rather than returning home early.

I remembered as the office clock finally approached the seventeenth hour, indicating it was time for the majority of my co-workers to call it a day, that everyone was anxiously waiting for the moment to get ready to leave in a mass exodus, or should I better describe it, in a "stampede" fashion. Another day in the calendar was gone where work was fully accomplished in the midst of tension and stress, but in an atmosphere of goodwill which would continue the next day... perhaps with feelings of anxiousness for some of us, like me, who are looking forward to keeping busy, and for others they might be less interested in coming back but are required, since we as perennial living creatures are dependent on our jobs in order to survive in this complex world.

As it was now a few minutes after almost everyone was gone, an atmosphere of tranquility was felt throughout the office. There were three of us who remained behind working late. I had to work later than usual because I was tardy for work today. Precisely I came in at 12:45 p.m., and as for the other two co-workers that stayed, they were freelancers with many years of experience at their professional trade. They had the option of working unlimited time in the office. I previously had notified the office secretary that I was going straight to the Outpatient clinic for a follow-up visit and might not be able to come back to work at all. When I first started to work in the Engineering office, I was allowed some sort of dispensation upon revealing my fictitious health issues. My boss Bernard Eblowitz, a public consultant engineer who happened to be the founder of the company, hired me expressing admiration towards me and displaying consideration for my health. For me, he was a model of a wonderful boss and was the epitome of success in his field. He was bestowed with such a terrific personality. He was dedicated and persistent in reaching the pinnacle of his professional career in this complex world. Having said that, I ended up demonstrating to him my high degree of loyalty for a span of almost seven consecutive years.

My doctor's appointment for this particular morning was for another intravenous medication. The chemical composition of this medication was extremely toxic and some of the side effects could include uncontrollable reactions followed by nausea. There was an endless struggle that was quite difficult for me to completely describe. It was a horrifying experience to feel its side effects once it was in my system. It was like feeling a sensation of being close to death. It was a difficult, traumatic state of mind, to say the least. From the moment the hypothermic needle penetrated through my vein releasing its chemical components, it would take between 5 to 6 hours for this medication's side effects to afflict my body.

So on this day after so many years of undergoing this systematic chemo procedure, I decided to go ahead and take chances. Instead of going straight home to rest to prepare myself for the worse side effects to come, I opted to go directly to the office since I wanted to make up for the time lost. I was aware of the serious consequence that may result from taking such a bold decision. So far everything was going well at my work; I was feeling good. However within fifteen minutes remaining before reaching the eighteenth hour, the time that I officially had previously set to finish my work, I started to get ready to leave the office, and for God's sake!, all of a sudden I started to experience some familiar mild side effects. Anticipating the inevitable that was to develop within me at any moment, I tried not to panic. I was trying to control with great tenacity the negative reactions I was experiencing. I was anticipating an embarrassing scenario that seemed eminent at any moment now. I obviously started gathering my work equipment and clearing my desk. My next move was to seek the door exit, but not without saying goodbye to my co-workers and wishing them a peaceful and pleasant night.

Once I left the office, I walked fast towards the subway station. This was located just one block away from the office, by the corner of Spring Street, and Lafayette Avenue, downtown Manhattan. There I was taking No. 2 Lexington line traveling north and transferring later to the F line subway east. I was traveling directly from the Borough of Queens to the 74Th Street subway station at Jackson Heights. This would be my last stop. While standing by the platform waiting for the train to arrive, I took notice of just how lucky I was since rush hour was over by now. This was a great deal of relief considering I was avoiding the typical pushing, and horrendous ritual hustle that takes place on a daily basis during rush hour. This was a really insane, almost diabolical, scenario that the majority of commuters unfortunately couldn't escape. My sympathy goes out to those victims of this caravan who I consider heroes for dealing with this nonsense week after week on a consistent basis.

Alas! While I was deep within myself recollecting my thoughts, the train made its triumphal arrival with an excruciating noise, something equivalent to twisting crushing metal. I looked up at the sky offering my thanksgiving to the Lord alleluia! As soon as the doors opened I rushed to grab any seat available. As I did, I leaned my back towards the seat to feel more comfortable. While the train was in full locomotion, all of a sudden it became notorious that my metabolism started experiencing butterfly-like feeling. This was related to mild stomach ache associated with nausea. This forced me to seek another quick alternative place to be within the train. In my quick thinking, it occurred to me to get out of my seat and seek refuge between the connections of the train car. This would be a perfect location to stay isolated from the rest of the commuters. In this way I could prevent an embarrassing situation. Meanwhile, upon accommodating myself in the imaginary trench, there reigned some sort of tremendous feeling of relief. I was a "bit" more comfortable even though I was anxious to reach my 'home sweet home' as soon as possible.

At this point I was praying to not encounter any unpleasant incidents along the way. I was in an almost perfect state of mind, meditating while preparing myself for the inevitable waterloo of sickness to hit me when a uniformed officer in a majestic fashion approached me and very politely started questioning me about my whereabouts in that area of the train. I had been standing between cars which was a violation according to transportation rules; only subway officials are allowed to stand between connecting wagons. After listening to him I expressed my deepest apology and proceeded to explain the reason why I was there. I continued in full disclosure explaining to him how I was developing circulatory discomfort associated with nausea symptoms. He told me I didn't have to create a grotesque scenario in front of other passengers by vomiting in front of them. In the meantime I reached out for my wallet, pulled my Outpatient Clinic identification card to show him I was telling him the truth. He felt sorry for me and gave me a pat on my shoulder wishing me to feel better. He then stepped back and disappeared into the next car. Am I a lucky person? Certainly indeed! A few minutes later the typical mild reactions started to increase with more frequency. However I was able to control it somehow with strong determination and mental will power. The side effects became more persistent to the point that I started again vomiting over a period of a few minutes. Chills took over my body and my body temperature rose. A profound sweating burst all over my body. I was lucky the subway was carrying only one third of passenger's capacity and that this happened while I was isolated. This made me somehow more comfortable, psychologically speaking. Obviously, there is no alternative to escaping from this horrendous ordeal. The battle was not over, I will soon start experiencing a series of reactions between convulsions and more nausea.

Finally the train had come to a stop. It arrived at the Queens Plaza Station. It would be a question of just minutes before the train picked up additional passengers who were transferring from Brooklyn. After a few minutes passed, suddenly the train started rapidly accelerating reaching a high speed into the tunnel directly traveling straight to the 74th Street - Jackson Heights station. Gladly, this would be my final stop.

Two things contributed to my already chaotic situation. My convulsions intensified and the train's fast motion didn't help me feel better. On the contrary this made me feel worse. I could hardly breathe! The first one was the loud noise the train created when its wheels had friction with the iron tracks. This was disturbing to me in a great manner. The other situation that bothered me was the strong wind created by the speed of the train passing through the tunnel. It was very difficult for me to deal with all of this at the same time. It was frustrating to see my inability to control all of the symptoms my body was going through at the moment. In my desperation I prayed to my Almighty Lord to grant mercies upon my soul and to allow me to reach my home as soon as possible.

After this huge battle in the train, my only consolation was to keep praying. I thought of the idea of going straight to bed to ease up all my symptoms and escaping this horrendous inferno that I was going through. My mind was thinking of sinking into a deep sound sleep, providing it will be the Lord's will. In an instant, Jiffy (the train), pulled into the station. This was excellent news for me. Taking into consideration the insurmountable frustration that I experienced that day, I honestly never wanted to live this situation ever again! The distance between my house and the 74th subway station was approximately a half mile. I considered this an easy walking distance for me when I was well; however, at this particular moment I was physically exhausted and in a lamenting state of mind. I felt awful. But I still felt lucky considering the worst was behind me.

While walking straight home, feeling as if I'm in the twilight zone, I was hoping to be alone without any pedestrians close by. However, when I was only a block away from the station I was forced to stop due to having convulsions again. These reactions were intensifying while I was experiencing nausea. Again I discharged tasteless fluid and a combination of medication and other components. At last I made my way home. As soon as I reached the threshold of the entrance door, I looked up to the sky and thanked the Lord for bestowing blessings upon this humble servant since I definitely wouldn't have been able to make it home without His intervention.

The house lights were turned off and an ambience of solitude reigned. I reached the conclusion that Clemencia and Ingrecita were not home and were probably with my mother in law, Helena. I walked into the kitchen, grabbed a can of chicken noodle soup, warmed it up and sat down to eat it. My nervous system was reminding me to nurture my body before contemplating going to bed. I didn't feel like eating anything at all, but I needed to get some strength back. I forced myself to have a few more spoonfuls of soup. After only a few minutes the inevitable happened again. I had to rush to the bathroom due to my queasiness. Convulsions followed and I was again battling this ferocious war against the side effects of the chemo. I realized that this night was going to take more than usual to recover. After each of my sessions of convulsions and other side effects were over, I proceeded to go back to the kitchen to try to finish my soup. Going through this ordeal made me feel very weak. I was wondering how much time had passed since my arrival, maybe 2 hours or more? I was not sure, but soon enough I finally found myself going to bed. I was completely exhausted and dizzy. I ended up losing touch with reality. Once my head touched the pillow, I passed out.

Usually each time I anticipated going through an ordeal of side effects after my chemo, I would ask Clemencia to spend that time with my in-laws so Ingrid would not have to be exposed to what I had to go through. Thanks to the Lord! I slept through the night and woke up fine. I was able to eat Clemencia's succulent breakfast. I felt completely restored to the point that Clemencia gave me a complement of how well I was looking. Soon it would be time for me to go back to work and to kissing my ladies goodbye for the day. There are not enough words to express my profound gratitude to my beloved wife for giving me unlimited physical and moral support during these difficult times of trial for me. I thanked the Lord for all of His blessings bestowed upon this humble servant. Amen!

After giving it much thought, I decided never again to go from the Outpatient clinic straight to work. What I had done turned into a complete fiasco and it was the last time I did it. Therefore I made a solemn promised to myself not to do it ever again, especially after having my chemo treatments.

During one of my visits to the Outpatient clinic, I was informed about a new sperm cell research program, which would provide information on how Chemotherapy might affect the sexual organs. This would be another alternative treatment for patients who were exposed to Chemotherapy for a long time. One of the medical assistants approached me requesting if I would like to volunteer for this new program. I had to bring to the clinic some of my specimens for the next two months while research was going on. He assured me that it will be a very simple procedure to follow since I shall be instructed how to collect, and cautiously handle it when commuting. Of course! My answer was an imminent "Yes!" followed by a big smile. I obviously felt good thinking of the idea that I could be a contributor to the cause, even though my contribution would be more likely compared to a drop in the bucket. Needless to say, considering that such request strictly was personal involving Clemencia and myself, I sincerely preferred trying to keep it confidential. Our mission successfully was accomplished, following the guide lines as instructed. Bottom line, it was admirable team work!

I instantly became very fond "from day one" of another sweet gal by the name of Helena, who, I must admit was "blessed" with personality and attractiveness. She was holding a position as Administration Assistant at the Outpatient Clinic Hematology Department. She originally immigrated to the United States from Europe, born in a Northern Italian city. A very gorgeous young lady possessed with beautiful physical attributes, besides a solid educational background. She was bilingual with several foreign languages at her command.

Whenever I came to the Clinic, she always would welcome me with a broad smile while uttering my name with her tender voice. I appreciated her spontaneous graceful attitude. In return, I would reciprocate, smiling while simultaneously blinking my eye, which she used to like because as time passed later on she told me so. On several occasions I had a delightful pleasure of joining her for lunch at the hospital cafeteria. I used to feel like a "million dollar" man, surrounded by strangers or some of those whose images we were familiar with one way or another, always they directly would smile, greeting us. Undoubtedly, I really was so proud just sitting next to her; I always yearned for these times of joyful togetherness. I was so lucky because on certain occasions I had a great deal of satisfaction escorting her to the subway station 5 blocks away from Memorial Hospital, but of course!, not before enjoying ourselves with a little "bit" of social life in the city. What unforgettable times we really used to have, indeed. I automatically used to become sad, sort of despaired, every time she would say to me "arrivederci William."

Aha! Rumors are circulating around at the outpatient clinic, particularly among staff members, and patients, as well, concerning a documentary on the agenda to be shown on a major television network station sometime in the near future. Obviously the topic content involves cancer cure's latest progressive crusade, which unequivocally is the second major undiscriminating disease affecting the human race worldwide. An alarming statistical result thus indicating why it is one of the leading causes of fatal mortality in the United States today. There will be a presentation illustrating how far along the successful progress of the Cancer research program has already been accomplished at Memorial Sloan and Kettering Hospital Center. Directors are studying whom to select among prospective patients for the interview soon to take place: an individual with long cancerous history, a Leukemia survivor who at present time still is in a stage of remission, preferably someone who has endured the longest surviving case history within the past five year period, which according to the latest medical official statistical records has not yet ever been reported until now. Doctors at Memorial actively are setting proper guidelines, coordinating how to proceed with the presentation thus making adequate arrangements, consulting with the television team crew personnel in charge, fully responsible for turning this awareness documentary into a complete memorable success.

The end dateline time is getting closer for doctors who will be assigned to participate in this documentary awareness project that probably will be seen by a large audience, millions of television viewers around the country and overseas. Well, after deliberating for a while, Doctors officially have reached a unanimous decision. The preceding medical researchers have selected me, quite an honor, to ultimately become a perfectly qualified model patient to participate in such an imminent television interview. The primary reason behind their unanimous agreement basically has been attributed to the number of years I have been in state of remission, over five years.

There is another patient, whose name is Jerry, who is nine years younger than me; he has been in remission for the past five year period, too. My kudos goes out to him because of the volunteer time he spent. He proudly has done some public commercial presentations in television, representing organizations involved in promotion of Cancer awareness. Having said that, blessed be he for his noble participation, henceforth, crusading live across the public broadcasting network.

As time was passing, I was engulfed in such uneasy curiosity just anxious to know the overwhelming determining factor in which I finally was able to become informed, as to why Doctors opted to select me among some other prospective qualified patients who also enjoyed a history of continuous state of remission. Therefore, the clear explanation that ensued next was strictly based on my personal statute, and long years of consistency reflecting my state of remission. Undoubtedly, they had considered as well my marital status, which I presently have been married for a period of five years, and my young daughter four years old, who has shown no symptoms or serious health issues. Nonetheless, they were taking into consideration that my wife's time of conception occurred during the first year, and precisely during the first stages that I was undergoing a chemotherapy protocol and being treated for Lymphoma type Leukemia.

I luckily had been accepted as a voluntary terminal patient still actively undergoing an experimental chemotherapy research program. Besides this commitment, I was presently holding a full time employment position, and simultaneously attending school after work. Also there was enough time dedicated, with a high intensity of discipline, to participating in different sports activities, something I proudly have enjoyed to the maximum of my desires, a full capricious obsession. This is the appropriate occasion, surely enough, to express that I absolutely have been blessed by my Almighty Lord above. Perhaps destiny had it that I still shall be around, because there is a task/mission that obviously must be accomplished prior to departing unto my everlasting voyage to eternity, God willing, Amen.

The date officially had been selected for going back for the anticipated national television network cancer documentary presentation. Therefore, a couple of days later, we received a call from the Outpatient Clinic secretary instructing us to come directly to Memorial Hospital early, somewhere around 10:00 am, for a preview introduction. Then, ipso facto, the official interview would follow with the scheduled date already set.

The long overdue day finally arrived; we really were looking forward to, quite excitedly, such a life's historical event. Upon hearing the alarm, we immediately woke up just on time. Meanwhile Clemencia and Ingrecita went through their early morning "last minute" personal vanity ritual, one that the majority of females characteristically and religiously practice and are infallibly fond of, perhaps with few exceptions to the rule anywhere on planet Earth.

I myself am engulfed in preparing a continental breakfast to appropriately start the day off physically fit, of course!, with a gentle smile on my face. And why not? Since we anxiously are anticipating what is approaching ahead, it might turn into a collective nervous breakdown indeed, which I hope will not be the case.

Once we are all ready and dressed, and seated at the dining table enjoying a well deserved breakfast, I could not help noticing how gracious they were. Before leaving the house, I sincerely expressed my courteous complement to them for they were looking so gorgeous now more than ever, just perfect for the special occasion which we shall be a part, participants at the main stage focus which was soon to take place this morning in front of television media coverage.

As we are stepping into the Hospital entrance, I could not help to take notice of an ABC television mobile armory vehicle parked in front of the main entrance and technical personnel hastily making last minute details. Of course! There was some sort of minor commotion as vehicular traffic almost came to a halt. Besides, by natural instinct, pedestrians were slowing down too while crossing, wondering, what in the "heck" was taking place, which famous celebrity had been admitted, discharged, or what else this might be about. Undoubtedly, my personal assumption which I find to be correct, is that this behavior is obviously a result of a typical human's distinguishable curiosity.

The moment of truth is near because as soon we exit the elevator, and we continue strolling directly towards the medical staff information desk control center, we are encountered by well wishers expressing words of encouragement in a friendly spontaneous atmosphere, including familiar faces, patients, and medical staff, as well as visitors or relatives who are accompanying some of the patients who had been previously scheduled for appointments this morning. There reigns such a nice ambiance of jubilee! I am starting to experience within myself a touch of celebrity, wow! It is not a question that I am trying to become pretentious, but it really is quite an emotional reaction for someone who is very humble, to say the least.

All of sudden, we come across the doctors and the television team crew members who extend to us a friendly welcome. Clemencia, Ingrecita, and I are touched by their display of appreciation towards us, thus with a great deal of pleasure we likewise respond to their spontaneous polite gesture. After a brief protocol introduction, we are instructed how the entire presentation will be conducted, therefore anticipating a complete success when the interview will have finally come to its conclusion. Once all last minute details were basically under control, it precisely was the appropriate time for the announcement: "testing once! Let's set the cameras ready to roll for action." The ceremony is about to commence, of course! Not before I am subject to a last minute sort of facial cosmetic treatment, making me feel just like a Hollywood "super late matinee star idol," ha! ha!

The moment of truth is eminent now, therefore no hesitation or turning back as we gradually start strolling across the corridor, slowly but surely with a gentle smile revealing an aura of jubilee but also engulfed with such mixed emotions, directly ahead to the area that has been properly set up for this unforgettable historical occasion. May I say with a high degree of certainty, indeed, that this event taking place is really becoming hilarious to me. Just to watch the camera crew performing their duty, acting in full harmony, focusing properly almost to the state of perfection, amazing to say the least. The gentleman who is doing the interview asks me if I am a little bit nervous, trying to make me feel comfortable. I entirely appreciate his benevolent intentions, a typical very professional approach of his own. My reply is almost instantly positive. I honestly feel quite comfortable, well beyond under control. I make a comparison that I am calm like a lamb. Having said that, he immediately begins a variety of series of questions, some of them about my persona, and others pertaining to my specific case involving my ailment. My medical history is an exceptional case reflecting a remarkable partial recovery, considering that I still am in a state of remission ever since the treatment officially was initiated dating back to March 1964.

After all the fanfare of the interview is finally concluded, there reigns an ambiance of pleasant brotherhood. I am being congratulated, and we all follow social ethics protocol stretching hands with gusto, congratulating each other with a high degree of optimism. And why not?, since it all has been done for a good cause, sending such an important message of awareness to the general public as to how medical science research programs have made a gigantic advancement in the battle against Cancer as we speak. Statistically, at present time, it is considered the second major illness with a high percentage of mortality cases. Hopefully our minuscule mission has been successfully accomplished, undoubtedly a justified reason for celebration, yes indeed.

In the meantime, as this scenario was taking place, I could not help notice my Ingrecita's little creature-like facial expression of surprise. My guess is that perhaps in her infinite innocence she was wondering what in the world was happening today, after being exposed for the first time in her infantile life to strange people, cameras, lighting equipment, and dad and mom being congratulated. As we are all almost approaching the "grand" finale, I do also take the opportunity on behalf of my wife and daughter to extend our most sincere appreciation, for such a terrific, wonderful experience for my family, and the unique opportunity to participate in this memorable documentary. It is obviously an honorable cause which makes me feel very proud, such a noble cause on behalf of the Cancer crusade throughout the United States of America. What an unforgettable experience we have been exposed to since early this morning. There is absolutely no doubt that this extraordinary event always will be remembered, an extraordinary day having occurred in our life's personal annals, indeed.

Something cute was happening on our way out as we were looking for the nearest exit from the Hospital complex center.

Along the way we encountered some persons who were aware of what had taken place by the Hematology Clinic, they came closer to congratulate, wishing us well, and some of them acting very funny requesting our autograph. Ha! Ha! Needless to mention how lovely the gracious spirit Clemencia and Ingrecita seemed to possess; nothing new or extravagant being said on my part.

For our first stop on the way, we thought it would be more than appropriate to walk into the Church, and express our gratefulness to our Lord all mighty God and request his blessings, amen! What a great feeling was the holy spiritual satisfaction once we were stepping out of the Church. Immediately after, we decided to stay together for a while, to treat ourselves with a well deserved lunch in the city, which usually is a case of joy indeed. Well, the time is running fast! Right after we conclude the succulent lunch that we immensely did enjoy, then we pause for a moment. Obviously the hour has arrived for us to say good bye, since it previously has been anticipated and well planned that I should be commuting straight to my office in order to make up for the time I took off this morning while having fully committed myself to appear on television speaking on behalf of the Cancer Research program at Memorial Hospital Center. Therefore, it would be a wise decision to go back to work to express sincere appreciation to my superiors for displaying a token of flexibility, whenever I have to be late or out of work for the rest of day, depending on medical necessity. Consequently it is quite appropriately planned to make up time for the remainder of the afternoon and early evening. It is obvious that it will make my boss quite surprised to see me coming to the office considering that previous day I already had requested a full day off. In the meantime, Clemencia already decided to stay with Ingrecita in the city for a short while, planning to take advantage of being there and to do some shopping. What is on her mind?

My guess is that it is obviously better not to ask anyway, just try to keep my "curiosity" in a low profile, nyuk, nyuk nyuk.

Something I did forget to mention is that after the documentary was finally concluded, I directly addressed myself to the news media staff asking them exactly when would be the date and official hour for the Documentary to be broadcasted on the air. They did not hesitate for a minute, instantly providing the information, and I quote "today sometime during the early evening news, and again tonight during the 11:00 P.M. late news presentation on channel 7 ABC network, New York, Eastern time."

Before wishing Clemenia and Ingrecita a safe trip back to home, I reminded them once again not to forget watching channel 7 ABC News early this evening, realizing that I shall be unable to return home on time precisely to watch it. Perhaps the only consolation would be later tonight after I had come back from work, in God's will. Well what a fiasco it turned out to be! As soon I arrived back to home sweet home, and during the course of having my dinner, I was listening very attentively to my "sweetheart" about how exciting it was to see us on television media, how stupendously we all performed, incredibly under control and living up to the occasion, and definitely somewhat short of phenomenal acting, maybe good enough for us to be selected nominees for the "Hollywood Annual Academic awards," ha! ha! ha! Upon finishing my dinner, by this time it was almost 9:30 P.M. I arose, walking away from the dining table, thus anxiously seeking refuge to my home's favorite place. Of course, where else but sitting quite comfortably in front of the television set, alert and fully prepared to listen to tonight's late news. Alas! What ensued next was not anything of major surprise at all considering I had had quite a stressful day filled with lots of activities since very early this morning, throughout rest of day, until coming back home from work later tonight. I really was so incredibly exhausted that as soon as I finally was able to accommodate myself and sitting quite comfortably, in a blink of an eye, revealing how exhausted I felt, it simply took a matter of minutes before I soundly fell to sleep for quite some time, and until my dear wife came to wake me right after the late news had already been reported. What a calamity, I said to myself, I missed such a great opportunity to watch myself on television. Who knows when there will be another opportunity, during my life time, definitely not in a zillion years, only The Lord knows best. Needless to mention, I directly confronted my darling about why she failed to wake me. Somehow, quite a bit prudently, her tender obvious reply was that since I promptly succumbed and deeply became in such a sleeping state, she "honestly" tried a couple of times to wake me up, however all was in vain. Well! There goes down the drain my chance of seeing myself on television media, perhaps completely vanished forever? Acta est fabula!

What a difference it really made, from the very first moment that I appeared in public, after being on a major Television network station. The instant popular celebrity status bestowed upon me obviously turned into major euphoria. Occasionally there was not any difference whom I was approached by between those who saw me on that particular night in front of the television screen, either relatives or friends, still they were able to recognize me somehow in my neighborhood, or some other public social circles. They all briefly took minutes of their own time, graciously extending sincere congratulations, also requesting my autograph, surely teasing me. My prompt response to their friendly spontaneous gestures was instantly reciprocating by expressing my gratitude with a great deal of affection, and a friendly broad smile typically indicative of appreciation. This was undoubtedly a unique personal experience, henceforth becoming part of my life's treasured memories locked very deeply in my heart, as long I am destined to live, so help me Lord. Amen!

S. O. S. - During the last days of summer in 1969, I physically experienced something very strange. It was on a day while I was commuting back home from work. I felt an excruciating pain in my body which lasted for less than ten minutes. I was very lucky this didn't happen while I was at work but it occurred just after getting off the subway from Jackson Heights Station, whose location was within a walking distance from home. Thank God the incident started as soon I was walking fast towards my place of residence. Suddenly I had to come to a full stop due to the intensifying pain. At this point, I opted to take my time going back home by resting until I felt comfortable enough to continue walking (to my final destination. I just wanted to arrive to my "home sweet home".

The following morning as soon as I woke up, I did not hesitate to call the Outpatient Clinic and report what happened to me the day before. While I was explaining in full details to the nurse on duty of the incident, she instructed me to remain at home and be calm. Undoubtedly I considered not going to work was the proper thing to do at the time. But, I waited until the nurse called me back to inform me about recommendations from the doctor.

The doctor had to review carefully my medical history before giving me any appropriate recommendation. Well, it did not take too long for the suspense to end for the phone rang after twenty minutes of waiting! There was not any doubt that this call was coming from the nurse of the Outpatient Clinic. As I reestablished my conversation with the nurse, she conveyed the Doctor's message by saying, "He (the doctor would like to see you Mr. Bulla. Come to the Hospital immediately if the pain comes again and intensifies. Otherwise, if there is not a recurrence of such a strange condition, then he will see you for your regular appointment in two weeks." Needless to mention, there would be additional observations and analysis pertaining to the mysterious pain I experienced that yesterday, early in the evening. I was very blessed that this incident was an isolated case, since there was not any recurrence whatsoever afterwards.

Alleluia! Encouraging great news arrived for me that coming Autumn Season. What was absolutely exciting for me was the terrific news I heard from the doctors. After reviewing my medical records, they reached a major decision considering my consistent progress and the persistent state of remission of the cancer disease. They were confident that with careful continuous monitoring of my health, I should be able for an indefinite time have my Clinic appointments less frequently than what they had been. Since 1964 I have been in remission from my cancer and this fact helped the doctors make their determination.

Thanks to the Lord for this to happen. What ensued next? Well! For the next six years I continued carrying on a normal life style without depriving myself from joyful activities that any other normal fellow would have. Following the rigorous chemotherapy research program that I was in, I responded quite well to all medications. I stayed in good physical and psychological health. After having deep and soul searching meditation with God, I definitely arrived at the conclusion that my All Mighty Father was not calling me yet to be in His presence. Nonetheless, I have been blessed by God zillions of times. He has bestowed on me the responsibility to carry innumerable missions into this complex World.

Year after year time was passing away leaving behind unforgettable memories from the medical point of view of my case. With my doctors, they always had a wonderful communication among themselves. Whether in good or critical times they always had an ambiance of mutual agreement in whatever situation was called for. A typical example of cooperation among doctors was when I was due for an intravenous medication in which my blood pressure was too low for such a procedure. It was perhaps quite risky for the medicine to be applied to me; however, after direct consultation with the Hematology Department Directors, Doctor Bayard Clarkson, who knew very well my medical history case as a patient, gave them his personal authorization for this procedure to be done. Dr. Bayard Clarkson was the supreme authority and was extremely knowledgeable in his field.

Another typical illustration of doctors reaching critical decisions pertaining to my treatments was when after careful review of my records they came to the conclusion of allowing an extension in the time between my appointments. As a result, my visits to the Outpatient Clinic were of less frequency than before. This suited me very well as time passed by. It was a great sign of recovery and it gave me hope that a cure would be developed in the future days to come. I expressed a profound gratitude towards the Almighty Lord for all of his blessings in my life from above. Amen.

A new chapter started to develop in my life when I heard from the Clinic staff and reliable sources that my odds for survival was quite unique! The progress of my conquering this disease was keeping the doctors very optimistic. They had become very impressed with my outstanding clinical results, which indicated improvement in my health as a response to the treatments given. The improvement was slow but sure with the greatest expectations never before registered anywhere in the medical field. Doctors involved in the cancer research program were not making any serious claims yet on winning the battle against Leukemia. However, there was hope created by cases like mine. The battle was still a long way from being declared a decisive victory. Meanwhile, doctors are being cautious, maintaining a good look at studies of conclusive research programs that have taken place in the medical field. A solution could possibly appear in the not so distant future. Doctors had arrived at the conclusion that a small number of patients had been able to tolerate the side effects of the Chemotherapy and or radiation, this only represents a small percentage of the survival rate. By the end of the year 1969 and according to statistics, only a few patients enrolled in the Cancer research program had been able to stay in remission stage for a period of 3 years or more. Unfortunately, countless patients have expired during their long struggle of finding the cure against this merciless disease. It was inexplicable to say the least.

On the family side of things, family stature becomes sort of a pride when a member seeks success in whatever endeavors he or she embarks on in life. An example of this was when our adorable daughter was growing up, maturing and becoming very successful in all of her sporting activities. At a tender age of 5 years old, she was doing remarkably well. Her great interest was participating in sport activities, and this was exceptionally worth Clemencia's and my admiration. She was destined to succeed in any sport that she found suitable to compete in. Take aquatics for example; she learned to master the skills just after turning 2 years old. At seven years of age, she was accepted to join the Nassau County Swimming Conference. Competing during a span of 6 years, she was chosen to be part of the Great Neck South Junior High School swimming team. During those years of competition she was not the most outstanding in her level. However, with her commitment, determination and excellent sportsmanship, she was a great contributor to her swimming team. This pleased me a lot because it showed that my chemo treatments didn't affect Ingrid at all. My wife became pregnant while I was still undergoing chemo treatments. My beloved daughter grew without showing any side effects of those treatment. Precisely in my early stages of cancer treatment, my wife and I were very romantically active when all of a sudden she became pregnant, by the grace of God. The rest is history.

From the year 1970 through 1975, I was bestowed with numerous blessings from Almighty God. I miraculously continued responding exceptionally well to the medication. Finally through time, my body began building immunity. I didn't have the typical convulsion-like side effects to the intravenous treatments. I was able to have better control over my day to day life. My faith became stronger than ever for as far back as I can remember. Let me clarify something, prior to this, even if being susceptible to trauma or intensive internal pain, I never for any reason showed signs of succumbing or contemplating cursing much less losing my faith. Faith was my strongest spiritual arsenal while battling this incurable cancer.

At times when I was in my recovery stage I would encounter some health issues, though nothing related to the disease itself. Anyway, on one particular occasion during the summer of 1972, while we were camping in the countryside, all of a sudden I experienced a tremendous acute pain exactly below the waist towards my right side. It lasted a long time, to the point that I threw myself to the ground to find some relief. Eventually the pain subsided but I felt my body's temperature increase to what felt like 100 degrees F. Somehow I was able to crawl inside the tent. I spent the rest of the night trying to recover from the pain. Clemencia and Ingrid decided to take a stroll to the Camp store where she encountered a nice couple; these people we met before. They recommended that she buy me a bottle of prune juice to ease up my discomfort. Later that same night, these nice people stopped by our tent to wish a good night. Clemencia told the lady, who worked in a health institution, all of the symptoms I was having that night. The lady arrived at the conclusion that I was probably having some calcium deposits in my bladder. Drinking the prune juice alleviated some of my pain allowing me to fall into a deep sleep until the next morning. I woke up feeling much better and we were able to enjoy the rest of the weekend at the Camp with no future health complication. From then on I was extremely cautious with my food intake. At the end we had a terrific time. Thanks again to the Lord's divine intervention, we came across that wonderful couple that gave us good advice. What a miracle indeed. I didn't feel the need to report this incident to any of my doctors. I felt quite well. But Bingo! Precisely 3 months after this scary incident, I was struck once again with another similar experience, but it was a different scenario.

This time it happened on a day, while I was at my place of work. I vividly remembered how it happened. I slid down from my chair unto the floor almost instantly when I felt the pain. I laid there for a few minutes until a co-worker spotted me and came to my rescue. He tried putting me in the best comfortable position possible and offered to call me an ambulance. Even though it was a very acute pain, I begged him to allow me to stay still until my pain would go away. Again with faith, and positive determination I was able to sit back into my chair and continue working until lunch time. The pain was disappearing little by little. My boss advised me to go home to relax and to call the doctor for future examinations. He was so concerned for me and I appreciated him very much for his wise advice. I could never forget his encouraging wishes for me to take good care of myself.

I arrived at the Outpatient Clinic and immediately underwent a full physical exam. The doctor in turn carefully reviewed my medical results and listened attentively to the description of my symptoms before the pain started. On both incidents, that of the camping trip, and the one at work, the pain came from below my waist area. The doctor concluded that I suffered from a calcium precipitation or stones. More tests needed to be done in order to have an accurate diagnosis. Meanwhile his recommendations were to drink lots of fluids, especially those rich in enzymes to help eliminate too much accumulation of calcium in my system. A couple of days later after seeing the results, the doctor diagnosed me with a bladder condition that had produced a high concentration of calcium carbonate. Thanks to the Lord, this was not related to any Leukemia symptoms. I was instructed to start taking some sort of medication for a brief period of time in combination with drinking fluids like cranberry, prune or pineapple juice. Well, this time good luck was undoubtedly following me! First of all, I did not have to undergo surgery to correct the problem. Secondly, I didn't have to subject myself to any emergency calls. I had subsequent isolated cases related with seasonal "allergies" like hay fever or an occasional encounter with an everyday virus, but never anything life threatening.

I was blessed during the 6 years between 1969 and 1975 with good health. I might have only had an occasional incident where I felt a little touch of physical discomfort due to my chemotherapy treatment. I considered this normal and didn't let it bother me nor disrupt my regular life activities. Year after year, I had the privilege to meet and interact with new patients who had been admitted to the Memorial Sloan Kettering Cancer Research Program. They all came from diverse ethnic backgrounds and or different walks of life. Some had come from far distant lands to be treated. But, we had something in common and it was the aspect of an uncertain destiny. In spite of the fact that at times there reigns a spirit of skepticism among us, the majority of my peers all possessed an admirable drive of positive thinking. They were strongly determined to follow whatever method it might take to become better, even if sacrifices were needed. They were all willing to do anything to reach their goal to live. For this their faith and determination had been the primary contributing factor of their drive to find a cure, without considering that the statistic of positive results would have been minimal. But without a doubt it was the dedication of the medical researchers, with their countless and exhausting hours which they spent trying to find the cure against this dreadful and devastating disease called cancer, for which I and others were so grateful. This had to be a monstrous task like comparing it to a missionary's challenge. Oh Almighty God! As a pilgrim of this world, I prostrate myself by your sacred feet pleading to you oh my Lord, to bestow countless blessings, wisdom upon doctors. Give them peace and to their beloved families as well.

One day during the summer of 1974 while I was having dinner with Clemencia next to me, and we were engaged in a casual conversation, Ingrecita, who was nine years old then, walked into the dining area and told us about the major events that transpired that day at the Great Neck Memorial Park. She explained to us that while she and some of her school friends were at the park, they had such a terrific time playing at the Park tennis courts; she found it quite fascinating to play tennis. She instantly fell in love with this sport. Needless to mention at that moment I became engulfed with exuberant joy, my emotions running high beyond belief. After listening to her personal experience she went through, I really reached the conclusion that this day would be a date to reckon with; therefore, from this moment on I did encourage Ingrid to pursue her aspirations. To me it was like a miracle in full swing. At that moment I felt like Ingrecita was going to live up to my dream of becoming a tennis player! This was a historical moment for me. She had all my support. I considered this to be nothing more than a miracle that I was being able to accomplish, through my daughter, one of my long desired dreams. I developed a passion for the game of tennis since I was five years old. It had become an obsession. Unfortunately due to financial reasons, my parents couldn't afford to support me for this activity. At that time, it was beyond my comprehension why my mother didn't pursue supporting me in my desire to play this game. Therefore with deep disappointment and sadness I accepted the fact of being unable to play tennis at all. Years later I came to realize that the sport of tennis exclusively was played either by elite or wealthy society. That said, always there were few exceptions to the rule.

As time passed, Ingrecita became very active in the tennis sport world, completely determined not to just learn, but also master the game. For my personal delight, her ambition was not just limited to being a recreational player. She went further beyond getting involved within her tennis activities; we ended up registering her in the Junior Tennis League program at a local tennis academy. Then the following year, she became a member of the Eastern Tennis Association, Long Island. District 6, New York. She escalated through the rankings with many meritorious achievements during her junior years. She successfully competed in her division level, and invitation tournaments. Alas! Time passed rapidly, and I became very much involved, partially coaching and assisting my daughter's training. My desire for her was to culminate the highest plateau possible within her tennis rank. I kept my mind so focused on her goals that it turned out to be a deterrent from thinking about my disease. And at the same time, I was gaining self confidence in my personal battle against cancer.

Having been afflicted by leukemia for almost a decade, focusing on my daughter's success in the sport had been like a therapy for me. I compared the positive effects on my health with Ingrid's accomplishments as if I was taking a good shot of penicillin. I felt blessed by being able to have distracted my mind away from my problem by focusing on Ingrid's successes.

Years came and passed 'like the blink of an eye.' My cancer still was in remission and life became as precious as ever. I was being blessed with relatively good health while still in the research program undergoing cancer treatments. Occasionally, I would be subject to some minor health issues like high fever during the months of May and September. Some symptoms made me feel extremely uncomfortable, for example, when I had days of sneezing all day and night due to allergy season. And, the occasional common cold would afflict me, but there was nothing major to worry about.

The doctors from the Memorial Hospital instructed me to abstain from consuming any non-prescribed drugs or vitamins for clinical records. I followed their instructions rigorously. Some exceptions to this rule would be medicine taken to alleviate extreme pain or discomfort. That said, I really never took any medicine at all, except cancer related. The doctors always reminded me that the reason for not taking vitamins and over the counter medicine was to prevent taking any additional medications, taking into consideration that my vital organs were being exposed to a protocol of extreme toxic drugs, and only time would be the best judge to determine the incalculable damage possibilities created by the treatment I was undergoing.

I, William, was becoming a celebrity by now within the community of medical researchers that held my case. I admired the dedication, devotion, and sacrifice that researchers gave in trying to find a cure for cancer. Results of their studies created an aura of tremendous hope and moral relief for so many millions of unfortunate people around the world afflicted by this devastating disease. It was obviously a question of time when the cure could be found by Almighty divine intervention. One day, in a not long distance future, this quest for cancer cure, finally would be converted into reality once, and for all on behalf of the human race, Amen!

Days, weeks, months, and years were rapidly passing by. To my surprise my cancer was still in remission. This puzzled many doctors from the Memorial Hospital. Some patients are stating that I am on my way to complete recovery. For how long? Nobody knew why nor did the doctors have an answer for this. However, their expectations from day to day were positive towards my case. I said it before and I'll say it again, having considered myself somebody who has struggled overcoming this mortal disease, what had helped me through all this years had been my perseverance and strong faith. As a matter of fact, I honestly believed after meditating that I had been bestowed with a special blessing from our Heavenly Father in Heaven by keeping me alive and healthy.

My regular daily life continued at the same pace, just by following the normal routine. There was nothing out of the ordinary, with the exception of periodic encouragement of positive news from the results of my medical treatment. Incredible it was to consider that it had been 10 years since my cancer has been in complete remission. Yet, doctors kept an eye on my disease and were very prudent when revising my latest medical reports. They had advanced in their pursuits to find cures. There was an official announcement stating that there was an optimistic outlook towards finding the treatments for some types of cancers. Meanwhile as time went by, doctors diligently were unrelenting in their work on this massive assignment as my life continued. I persisted to be involved in many private and public affairs fulfilling my daily obligations with a happy heart.

Sadly, during this 10 year period of my life, I saw patients come and go through the Cancer Center. They actively participated in a research program, but unfortunately the majority of them ended up succumbing to the disease itself or experiencing the horrible side effects of the medicine.

Starting from this unforgettable date of which I reckoned with, and I am referring to March 21, 1974, straight through the following year culminating on June 18, 1975, my Outpatient Clinic's regular appointment visits officially became somehow less frequent; therefore more flexibility of my time than previously recorded was available since I first started the Chemotherapy volunteer research program dating as far back to April, 1964. Now, almost 10 years later, it is hard to believe how rapidly time passed; "it seems like it was only yesterday;" that is exactly my typical expression whenever I am referring to how fast time passes by. Precisely! This month of March 1974, it has been quite exactly a decade since I undoubtedly was bestowed with blessings from above, especially during this long life expanse of time, when I was partially responding exceptionally well to preliminary medication which catapulted me at that moment into the state of remission. And for the Lord's grace, destiny had it that I should consistently continue without any unpredictable interruption during this critical period of my life and extend year after year.

Therefore, doctors at Memorial Hospital who were directly involved in the Cancer research program, unanimously decided that it would be appropriate enough, quite convenient, to start eliminating the rigorous schedule of visits and procedures that I was solemnly following until then. Thus a day arrived when I was directly informed by the doctors of their good intentions of setting a more flexible protocol on my behalf. It was very important for them to make a risky decision in order to find out how I would continue to respond to less stressful conditions like fewer bone marrows, less exposure to X-rays, and some other laboratory sample texts etc. From that moment on when I first started to undergo the new schedule protocol that ensued next, it was magically soul lifting for me because I practically was coming to the clinic only every other month. I was myself delighted, and obviously for a good simply reason, now I was spending more time working, and being more productive and efficient in my office professional endowments. From the financial point of view it really was very gratifying, since I was able to concentrate much better on my obligation. From an ethical point of view, I was able to reduce my efforts in trying to make time to cover up for my lateness or taking time off from work whenever the occasion called for it.

Months came and went like the blink of an eye, and I was enormously thrilled, for the simple fact that days, weeks, and months ahead irrevocably continued without any complication or setbacks for me to lament dealing with my health issue statute. On the other side of the coin, I must admit that whatever I was traditionally more frequently accustomed to in my daily physical and psychological routine, I started to miss. Definitely I am not being sarcastic at all, just because of the fact I do reminisce the golden days when there reigned a spirit of cordiality among all of us patients, and the medical staff; so much display of camaraderie was the order of the day. Every time I went to the outpatient clinic for observation, in spite of our serious adversity we were lucky enough to find time to chat, tell jokes and laugh during the time we were waiting to be called. For my own personal experience, obviously it became another chapter of my life then, which I presently am starting to miss immensely, awfully indeed. Well! Time keeps marching on and I definitely have to properly adjust for what I will be confronting ahead and beyond; besides I must humbly appreciate what the Almighty God has chosen for this world's pilgrim, Amen.

There is something personally revealing that it is worth mentioning concerning the treatment and new visit schedule. It is certainly true that as time passed since commencing the new revised outpatient clinic calendar scheduled visits every other month, psychologically my attitude once and for all took a negative turn, particularly related to common procedures. Thus let me be more specific, giving you a typical illustration. For example, back during the first years after I became part of the Cancer voluntary research program, which continued for over a decade, I got accustomed to being complaisant to certain discomforts or agonizing procedures, therefore becoming familiar with the strong side effects, particularly to some of the toxic drugs whose characteristic sign was inducing severe convulsive reaction in the metabolism. Let's take for instance, whenever bone marrows were required that used to be performed constantly, or the two spinal chord tap tests, undoubtedly the most feared medical procedure, the unforgettable excruciating pain exceeded all other kinds of agonizing pain that my memory could recall ever having before in my life time, going way back to infancy. The anesthesia that used to be applied to minimize the pain, or discomfort for that matter, or the strong toxic drug that I was taking intravenously every two months year after year, quite frequently would induce me to have a very strong **nausea tic** condition, needless to mention upsetting my metabolism system. It is difficult to comprehend the nostalgia of these events which theoretically, to begin with, were not too pleasant, however, it is purely indicative of my personal experience. I was not going to be seeing the doctors, nurses, or other medical staff, and patients. I was going to miss the religious and public places which I used to enjoy and stop by quite often, also streets and corners where I regularly used to cross walking on my way to the Hospital. Also, let's not forget some of those citizens whose faces became very familiar as years came and went for such a long time period, always greeting whenever we came across each other, reigning an atmosphere of jubilee, a spirit of friendship indeed. It is incredible to believe that all of this personal experience turned out to be exactly a traditional routine period of time. Therefore, by more frequently missing this incumbent traditional sequence just the way it used to be, somehow sooner or later as expected this drastic transition of events obviously resulted in creating a deep spiritual combined state of anxiety and nostalgia to my soul.

Of course, deep in my heart there is no any negative contemplation concerning my latest medical schedule change. On the contrary, I really am immensely content with a great deal of joy, taking into consideration that from now on if I do continue being blessed in a stage of remission, the question mark is obviously, how long would it be? The answer, only God knows until when, but in the meantime I shall conduct myself with a high degree of confidence and determination overcoming any psychological problems that may arise within myself.

Now realizing I am going to have more ample time especially to accomplish certain family affairs, for instance, I shall dedicate more time to my daughter's sport activities, who by the Lord's grace at present time has physically grown quite rapidly, is psychologically wiser, and enjoys a terrific personality, great scot! I realize very soon she promptly will be celebrating her 10 year birthday, providing it is the Lord's will, Amen. Speaking about her latest tennis developments, undoubtedly she really has gone beyond her expectation, exhibiting her potential with a great deal of confidence, her super excellent talent devotion, and self-determination and drive to accomplish future tennis interscholastic endeavors. Only with time for sure, we shall know whether or not she will reach the zenith of her dreams indeed. As a father obviously I am deeply confident that with a profound sign of faith, countless prayers, and little bit of luck, Ingrecita's destiny will be a success; therefore, in God's will in a not long distance future, shall I survive to witness it? Perhaps, the remote possibility still is uncertain as time will passes.

One day when I was coming back to the outpatient clinic, precisely my second scheduled appointment since the beginning of the year 1975, as soon as I registered at the front desk control center, I went looking for a spot to sit and wait until being called. I accommodated myself quite nicely on a very plush comfortable couch at the public waiting reception area next to other patients who I usually engaged with, enjoying such an ambience of camaraderie, always involved in friendly conversation. Alas! It was then that I heard some interesting rumors, previously disclosed, now once again back in circulation; I am referring to some personal comments by a doctor during a medical conference. He had arrived at a conclusion, after a series of serious evaluations on my medical recovery progress, indicating how quite remarkably well and consistently my system had been able to respond to the medication, thus an excellent reason why I was still in a stage of remission for such a long time period, never before registered for an expanse of 11 years, to be precise. Therefore, some of the present time rumors circulating around perhaps have been taken from highly reliable sources, and I quote what I heard: "patient William Bulla with a long Cancer history, lymphoma leukemia, has been officially in the voluntary research program, for a definable time period, and still under the same protocol of medication, and his response has been sort of remarkable, very encouraging news," said that, "he undoubtedly is a perfectly selected candidate to be released from any further Chemo medication dependency." Upon hearing these rumors, obviously I did not take it so seriously, considering the fact that on a previous occasion, I already had heard similar comments, yet at that time or even after, there were not medical records to substantiate any medical official report to stop action as far as the chemo termination was concerned.

Right before concluding the Clinic's regular visit observation, during that time, I definitely did not hear any type of comments by the doctor during the examination procedure, nor any speculation review concerning the latest medical studies done on patients who have been at a stage of remission for quite a number of years so far.

According to rumors, medical researchers are seriously debating which direction or alternative to ensue next, taking the necessary maximum precaution in deciding which of those patients may be qualified for selection based upon expectations of positive response which could ultimately establish a free dependency from any further Chemotherapy. I am not too anxious or qualified to confront the Doctor with any interrogation to confirm the validity or dismissal of those rumors circulating around in full swing. Once and for all, I arrive at the conclusion that for my own sake it is better off to let the doctors decide when the right time will arrive in order for us to be officially informed; in the meanwhile let's be prudent about this crucial mandate.

As I was leaving the hospital I came across Doctor Timothy Ma, who I had not seen for quite some time; it was a nice and brief encounter since he was on his way out for lunch. However we a few minutes to express our pleasure of seeing each other; it was then that he did rapidly mention the euphoria I was creating among the medical field. He said that I have been doing extremely well, showing remarkable progress during the past 11 ½ years. Therefore, doctors are satisfied with the progress in my latest medical records. Based on this, they will soon make a decision to exit me from the program. I was so excited and delighted to listen to Dr. Ma's comments. Saying goodbye to him, I expressed my deepest gratitude for this news.

Doctor Clarkson's appointment finally arrived two weeks later. I came to the Hospital just on time, but must confess I practically was experiencing so much anxiety that my nervous system was almost reaching a breaking point; it really was something abnormal, never before I had any recollection of this reaction, per se.

Once inside the Hospital I followed my traditional ritual, greeting, smiling, waiving, and wishing well to everyone I came across whose persona I was familiar with. Immediately after undergoing registration procedures, I was instructed to take a seat and wait for the doctor's eminent arrival. It really turned into long agonizing moments, perhaps because I was feeling extremely anxious, and there was a good reason why, considering today's meeting would be a crucial determining factor concerning my future destiny.

Before you know it, all of a sudden Doctor Clarkson, with his imposing unique personality, makes his entrance to the Hematology Department visitor's waiting room. I instantly reacted by standing straight up, and acknowledging his presence. He really has been such a profound inspiration to my soul throughout these struggling years, ever since I first met him back in year 1964. After shaking hands, and with a broad smile typical of his, we took a short walk into one of the adjacent private rooms, and he formally asked me to take a seat, and make myself comfortable while he proceeded to close the door for complete privacy. Once he casually took his seat behind the desk, he immediately started asking me how I have felt lately, how my family is doing - especially my daughter Ingrecita, how she is doing in school, believe or not! But psychologically I am starting to react much better, more comfortably indeed, realizing that the moment of true inevitably is near. My anatomy already is getting under control; that said, he restarts his conversation with a firm sense of authority, thus establishing reference to a brief historical recollection of events that has occurred over a decade and how advantageous and beneficial the chemo program has been up to this date. That said, he immediately starts explaining the reason for this meeting, and I quote him saying: "William, starting from this date on we have decided to release you from undergoing any further Chemotherapy, therefore, no longer depending on medication. You continuously have been in a stage of remission for such a long time period, ever since September 1964, and during this time you have shown such a remarkable steady recovery, which undoubtedly make you a perfect candidate. Also we are very much concerned with some of your internal organs that eventually might bring some negative repercussions from being exposed to the strong medication. There is a tremendous possibility you will be able to stay free of symptoms that have the potential to occur, thus only time will tell. However if for any reason you go back out of remission, please do not become panicked, because you immediately will be admitted into the Cancer program, and exposed to the latest protocol of medications."

That said, the interview reached conclusion, however he wisely advised me that I must have a bone marrow test done before leaving. Besides that, we must have a celebration, and for the Bloody Mary's toast, some ingredients highly are required. Of course, some of my bone marrow blood would be used in lieu of tomato juice. Ha! Ha! Little did I know that it would be the last time I would see Doctor Bayard Clarkson; he always will be in the deepest part of my heart for as long I might live. For the record, I must admit, I did try numerous times to request a personal interview with him years later, but all was in vain because he previously had requested his privacy upon his retirement. I really miss him immensely, to say the least.

The years are passing incredibly fast, similar to celestial bodies traveling beyond and across the Milky Way, undoubtedly reminding us terrestrial creatures that time flies and therefore making us realize that life is a dream, too. What spiritual indulgence I have profoundly experienced today, after having spent a moment of meditation, but especially paying the Lord respects for His goodness, and humbly expressing thanksgiving to Almighty God for partially restoring my health, thus strengthening myself with a great mist of hope, and my will to overcome adversity. At this stage of mind, I really feel like I'm carrying a flame torch as an emblem of strong profound faith. During this time also, I do solemnly promise my Lord: although I shall not be coming to the Hospital any more on a regular basis, whenever I may be crossing this vicinity I shall step into the Church to pay my respects, thus traditionally continuing the holy practice as long as the Lord Father has traced my life's destiny on Earth.

In the meanwhile, as I directly proceed walking in silence forward through the center alley, seeking the Church's main door exit, all of sudden I unintentionally start experiencing mixed emotions, realizing it has been over a decade since I first started stepping into the Lord's house, undoubtedly the Holiest refuge center, source of worship, solitude, and inspiration for my weary Soul, thus no better place of choice for renewing my faith strong conviction. After having spent some time deeply in meditation, upon concluding my time was up to retire, suddenly, just like a blink of an eye, I proceed to trespass the church door threshold into the exterior, joining the world's mundane transient caravan where soon I found myself walking along the way, joining the rest of the human masses. Interesting peculiar scenario, characteristic of minuscule hard working ants actively engaged, consistently moving in such a hasty fashion, each individual ant performing its missionary task running back and forward to their designated destination, of course! They really conduct themselves in a more orderly fashion than us "rational "creatures, hmm?

I continue crossing city block after city block, which by now I already have become quite familiar with since back to April 1964. As I am walking, concentrated on recollecting my thoughts, I am simultaneously sightseeing as well. It reminded me of such unforgettable places I frequently used to visit, stopping to relax, make a purchase, or just simply socially interacting, besides enjoying having lunch or a refreshment. Nevertheless, throughout these years, when I frequently used to walk to or from the Hospital, I had great fortune meeting people from all walks of life. As time passed, and their faces became familiar, after a while we warmly established among ourselves a cordial camaraderie. There is no question about it that mother's caring personal intuition on my persona was a major factor. During early stages of my adolescent life she created an enriched strong family root value foundation basically being a major contributor to my positive results, undoubtedly a typical reflection of how my upbringing really was during those preceding days. Therefore one of my life's major spiritual accomplishments has been able to incumbent a unique inspirational image, thus gaining anyone's personal confidence, and their trust as well, which resulted in an unequivocal precedent of auspicious communication channels.

Considering how fast time was passing, I finally decided it would be better off staying around midtown Manhattan and enjoying a little bit of the ambience this city area has so much to offer, rather than directly commuting to my office just to work a few hours, which I realistically found impractical and somehow worthless. Without further ado, I said to myself that I may as well celebrate this unique occasion for the rest of afternoon, whatever time still remains. Who knows whether or not it may be my last time strolling around this city area? Only Our Lord Jesus Christ knows best what the future holds for me. Honestly clear, that is how convincing my rational was. Obviously, I firmly arrived, concluding it was the right selected decision. Let me tell you that I graciously enjoyed every single hour which I spent this late afternoon, of course!

Since I already was aware of the hassle and inconvenience during commuting rush hours, I purposely took action trying to avert any complication. Thus I wisely decided to start getting ready to return home earlier than traditionally accustomed, trying to avoid the hectic rush hour indeed. "Good bye to Broadway" was my selected farewell theme as I started to walk directly across to the Lexington Avenue subway station by the 59th Street entrance on my journey back to home sweet home. In the meanwhile, as the train pulled out of the platform station traveling at a high speed in locomotion across the tunnel, I became quite engulfed in reminiscing about a series of major events that occurred at the Hospital earlier this morning, especially the tremendous revelation news by Doctor Clarkson, concerning my future days ahead, officially being discharged from the Cancer Research Program, therefore medication free. Undoubtedly, another day on planet Earth, to reckon, the rest of my life to say the least.

It is hard to believe how time passes so quickly, especially when the calendar indicates that very soon the Doctor's clinic follow up appointment is approaching, 4 months after my release from the program, therefore reminding me once again I shall contact the Hospital for official confirmation. I had been instructed to suspend the treatment rather than prolonging it for who knows how long, and eventually developing irreparable organ damage. It will be most important to report a personal account of my experience, particularly concerning whether any significant irregular symptoms associated with the disease which might have developed during this trial period.

I had confronted a new scenario, living an ordinary life entirely free from taking Chemo medication drugs any longer, as long I was in a stage of remission. Amen. For quite some time, I really had anticipated going to the Hospital and delivering to the doctors an encouraging news report of what has transpired throughout this time period.

As I rapidly am walking straight to the bus stop to go to my appointment, something struck my mind in a matter of seconds. I realize that it has been quite a long time since making my last trip to this exact destination four months ago; hard to believe how quickly time goes. I took the number 21 bus from my neighborhood in Great Neck, Long Island, directly to the bus's last stop at Flushing, Queens, New York, then continued a short stroll to IRT Subway Station. Last stop. Suddenly I find myself stepping into the escalators down to the platform, taking the subway train to the borough of Manhattan. Once I had reached the trains last stop destination, then from there I shall be walking 5 blocks cross-town straight to the Hospital's main door entrance.

On route to the Hospital, I always had the option of taking the city public bus transportation, or just a short five block walk. Today I have selected to exercise a little bit, therefore I prefer to walk; besides the weather is just fabulous. As I am walking across town, I could not control my sentimental emotions while reminiscing that it was not too long ago when I frequently used to stroll across this area of the city, precisely from the early part of Spring season 1964, when I first became admitted at Memorial Sloan-Kettering Cancer Center undergoing a treatment for an incurable disease Lymphoma leukemia. Four months have passed since the last time I was strolling around this area; however I did not notice any major changes, per se. As a matter of fact, all local stores, restaurants, etc., still were open for regular business; everything seems to conform to the city's traditional daily routine. Perhaps there were a couple of new commercial establishments, otherwise all still conducted under normal operation. Another interesting observation is how the city still manages to maintain its vibrant atmosphere, as well as the progressive development projects so far successfully accomplished by our city's municipal officials, politicians, and urban leaders. That said, quite surprising that our taxes have been well implemented!

At last! Memorial Sloan-Kettering Cancer Center's prestigious edifice is in sight as soon as I am turning around the corner on 68th Street and York Avenue, just a short distance away. I find myself once again in front of the Hospital's main entrance, after such a long time. I must confess that my heart is going like a "yo-yo," swinging up and down. I am so thrilled returning again to MSKCC, which I have come to realize had become my second official residence for more than a decade. After months of absence, my personal impression definitely is positive, all still is the same daily routine. A contingent of patients with personal health cases cross through the main entrance seeking, like a last resource, some relief for whatever degree may be their agonizing condition. Unfortunately, the irony of life is that by the time a great number of patients struggle trying to recover from their illness, other patients in the meanwhile have given up, completely losing hope to their cause, and standing outside in front of Hospital's main entrance they succumb to the deadly habit of smoking cigarettes, perhaps seeking some sort of relief, a panacea to their miseries. Only God knows the real truth of their destined fate, very sad indeed; they dare mother nature, and practically do not give a damn ignoring all imaginable consequences that imply fatidic end results. At the opposite scenario, others like myself, or in worst health conditions imaginable beyond belief, are more likely entangled in suffering with their fateful destiny, however inspired with a profound faithful determination to overcome the most lamenting stage of their lives, still struggling for survival at least another day, in their endless battle against the fatidic Cancer disease. Such is life that is my assumption. Amen.

Incredibly, it is veridical that for several months I have experienced some sort of suspense scenario, and I particularly am referring to a personal dilemma I am confronting, but obviously seeking to resolve hopefully soon. Precisely right after my chemo program recently was terminated, and the clinic follow up visits became less frequent, quite contrary to previous traditional every other week visits for over a decade, it was exactly then, with the latest events, that I decided to take a very deep soul searching.

Thus what were the end results? I seriously contemplated and reached what I consider one of the most critical decisions I have confronted in my entire life. It basically encompassed an imminent consideration, a strictly personal decision of mine, to faithfully continue living a simple normal life. I shall introduce a low profile recommendation during my doctor's participation in discussing my future health projection. Obviously once his consideration has been carefully determined, and officially instituted, my concern was starting the soonest possible.

Therefore the more practical course henceforth to follow was contemplating a simple, idealistic scenario. Undoubtedly, taking into consideration case options, I became more inclined to stop coming to the hospital's follow up visits any further. It was preferable, reaching a practical solution, to seek a highly qualified neighborhood doctor who semi-annually would perform a full physical exam, following Memorial Hospital's medical protocol of course providing that I should be completely free from any symptoms, and actively continue to be physically healthy, in other words spiritually blessed while still in a stage of remission, indeed. That said, the crucial question is if I am confident enough, quickly counteracting any negative reaction, and still capable of confronting any sort of complications resulting from stubborn symptoms that might reappear, once again spreading out of control. Of course, technically speaking, this definitely represents a high risk to reckon with, yet with no room for hesitation. I really feel quite confident in myself, making an "ultimate" decision if it calls for one. Needless to mention, the major important factor at this stage of my life is, staying positive. Reaching this conclusion, why not consider extending this time period to almost a year, since medical records clearly indicate that I have been completely free from medication and undergoing chemotherapy sessions? Besides, the common denominator indicating really encouraging facts is that up until present time, I still am in a stage of remission, uninterrupted going back as far as October 1964, following a brief 3 month's relapse period, when I first was struck with illness, and subsequently became enrolled in a voluntary research program. There is no question that I definitely have been blessed from above, and for my own sake typical trace symptoms from Lymphoma Leukemia Cancer disease has never reappeared again, as far as medical history records thus may indicate. My Lord and Savior, humbly prostrated on my knees, please accept my profound thanksgiving offers for Your blessings bestowed upon myself, humble pilgrim of this World. Amen!

Once my follow up visit to the outpatient clinic was approaching, and considering how miraculously well I physically was responding to expectations, aside from my state of anxiety which I am experiencing, a factor that rapidly was growing a little bit unusual as days were approaching, the urge to meet the Doctors at once was really turning into something pretty anxious. I could hardly wait any longer for the sought after meeting, and anxious to express my own personal recommendation concerning my future health care projection; a simplified presentation considering the magnitude of its nature, consequently soon to be adopted.

Well, before you know it, the day I had anticipated finally arrived. How excited I really was, and why not? It was time to soon start getting ready, and commute to Memorial Hospital for my follow up appointment. In the meantime, as I was in the process of preparing now to leave home, something serious crossed my mind. I was fully aware that it might be my last follow up visit to the clinic since almost a year ago when the Doctors unanimously decided to terminate the long lasting treatment, which I previously came short of describing as perpetual, per say. As I vividly remember, on this particular day I suddenly woke up half sleepy; looking directly through the window I could see how clear and bright a sunshiny morning it really was, which I could perfectly describe as invigorating to the soul indeed. Then what ensued next? When the radio alarm sounded, thus by natural instinct I instantly jumped out of bed, and proceeded to follow my childhood traditional meditation practice, something of great spiritual value. My mother's intuition inculcated, and wisely encouraged me to continue this spiritual ritual practice with the Lord on a daily basis, the zenith beginning of a new day, foremost with the Lord's presence always in one's mind. Therefore, prostrated on my knees in front of Thee Heavenly Father, I started to offer my prayers, requesting for special petition, and offering my thanksgiving to the Lord for all his blessings, strengthening my will, and purifying my soul, Amen!

The moment of truth has arrived, and is here to stay. I am referring to the sought after meeting with Doctor Gee whose principal objective precisely was to discuss and resolve the crucial dilemma that insensibly has haunted me time after time. Therefore the long sought after meeting at Memorial Hospital officially arrived, turning into reality just like I anticipated. Suddenly I found myself standing in front of Doctor Timothy Gee whose intense dedication, major contribution, and remarkable personal record of his crusade battling the Cancer disease in pursuit of the ultimate cure, had set him recently apart on a high plateau. He was unanimously chosen among his colleagues, thus attaining the highly respectable and admirable leadership position, substituting for former Doctor Bayard Clarkson as Chief Director of the Hematology department based on his immaculate credentials portfolio, and distinguishable professional medical career that originally started back in his native country, Republic of China.

Once laboratory blood test results were completely done, they immediately were delivered to Doctor Gee for his personal analysis. Upon reviewing the entire report, he found it very encouraging, quite satisfactory; he really expressed an aura of high optimism, not to mention how he obviously was impressed by the positive results. Besides let's take into consideration, too, the recent determining factor of suspending my chemotherapy treatment all together, in lieu of a new protocol projection; this was based on a well calculated decision made by the doctors after carefully reviewing my medical history and being released from the chemotherapy research program. To everyone's amazing surprise, I have miraculously survived partial recovery of this devastating disease, which I have been able to overcome for more than a decade. Undoubtedly professing my personal motto: "I must have faith in God, faith in the doctors, and faith in myself."

Prior to concluding the follow up visit, I decided to directly address to Doctor Gee some of my composed questions pertaining to uncertain related health issues unto future projections, thus anxiously waiting to listen to his personal evaluation involving what I characterize as major issues. The first, and perhaps most important, concerns my health's history statute. I lately have been experiencing a psychologically tormenting struggle as to whether or not after all these twelve long years, estimating my health history case and consistent stage of remission, it would be sufficient enough for Doctor Gee and research doctors to consider that by now I have reached a plateau, an indicative sign of recovery from this fatal dreadful disease Leukemia, of which I severely was afflicted long time ago, during my life's earliest years. It really is incredible to realize how <u>fugi</u> time has passed; therefore without any tantalizing, I immediately proceed by questioning him about any remote possibility of being declared automatically cured. Obviously following a brief suspense, taking deep breaths, his response was very tactfully illustrated by explaining to me that medical researchers were extremely cautious in announcing some of the latest radical advancing discoveries. Not until more statistical cases similar to mine had been reported would they be taking any serious initiative in publicly declaring tremendous positive achievements towards a decisive victory battle in the crusade to strike out cancer in our life time.

He also went as far as explaining crystal clear that my case has been quite unique, an exceptional case. Undoubtedly it has been considered somehow not less than a miracle by all accounts. However I am not alone in the survival quest list because besides myself, encouraging news is circulating around there about another surviving patient with similar symptoms who also was admitted some year after 1964 at Memorial Cancer Center in the leukemia research treatment program, undergoing similar protocol of medication, except occasionally exposed to an additional sort of radiation session. In my chemo protocol program I never was exposed to radiation sessions. Out of the unfortunate thousands of patients who underwent radiation, sooner or later they succumbed to the disease or perhaps to the rigorous devastating treatment implementing toxic chemo drugs, and radiation combined, but only two of us who have survived such an ordeal have been blessed with overcoming such a mortal disease, better described in the medical encyclopedia as Leukemia Cancer of the blood.

The second critical part concerning my health issue by all accounts, would encompass a great deal of mutual compromise between the Doctor and myself by seeking to reach an agreement, thus ending our conversation with a highly optimistic outlook displayed beyond the unpredictable future. There is no doubt in my mind, and I am quite confident, that I am going to be comprehensible for this particular case, and that he will graciously display flexibility once he has finished listening to my recommendation, which I already had diligently prepared not long ago. Now finally time is appropriated for me to introduce my proposition to the doctor for his review. In conclusion, I am very confident expecting that my propositions would simply enough sustain an agreeable decision, thus an encouraging effort, providing it will be favorable accepted. Undoubtedly, it will be a major factor dictating my future.

As previously mentioned above, the second recommendation constituted simply seeking professional service from a doctor in my neighborhood who would be performing a complete physical examination semi-annually, of course providing that my body shall endure life's intricacies, complex challenges, which are part of the routine one confronts day after day. Another very important fact that must be taken into consideration is financial, involving medical bills expenditures. A typical example would be cost per visit, which in my calculation would definitely be a substantially less demanding expense, more reasonable, with a reduction in the number of doctor visits. A great deal of time flexibility, as far as the appointment visit schedule is concerned, is another beneficial consideration.

Alleluia! Alleluia! That was my spontaneous exclamation, almost jumping for joy shortly after listening to Doctor Timothy Gee firmly declaring his final resolution, thus concluding the visit's follow up by reaching full agreements to my proposals. He went further emphasizing how he finally had arrived at his ultimate determination, thus obviously accepting what I already had categorically considered my critical recommendation: a firm emphasis combined with a display of confidence, and undoubtedly the practical approach to ensue next under such unpredictable expectations beyond, providing that I should be in stage of remission as long as I am destined to live. Thus if I am blessed, and otherwise survive the ordeal, then obviously I arrive at the conclusion that there is not cause without a fundamental reasoning for which I have survived, and have been definitely chosen to fulfill a spiritual mission on Earth, according to The Almighty Lord's divine plans, Amen.

Upon concluding what I really came to consider perhaps my last follow up visit to Memorial Hospital, all I can utter out immediately after farewell's final minutes is "Incredible." This was marred by an exuberant expression of mutual emotions among all of those who I was fortunate to encounter, while on my way out before leaving MSKCC. It really was such an unforgettable life experience to say the least; there reigned the warm spirit of brotherhood's action, a diversified display of composed expressions appropriated for the occasion, like sincere "best wishes," thunderous "warm congratulations," and "good luck in your future." These were just a few of the friendliest good will messages to mention; undoubtedly, it is part of sweet treasured memories that shall remain deep in my Soul for the rest of my life, Amen.

Oh, Lord, please! Enlighten my understanding, strengthen my will, purify my heart, and keep my faith stronger, until my last day on Planet Earth. Iact est fabula. Almighty Father. Amen.

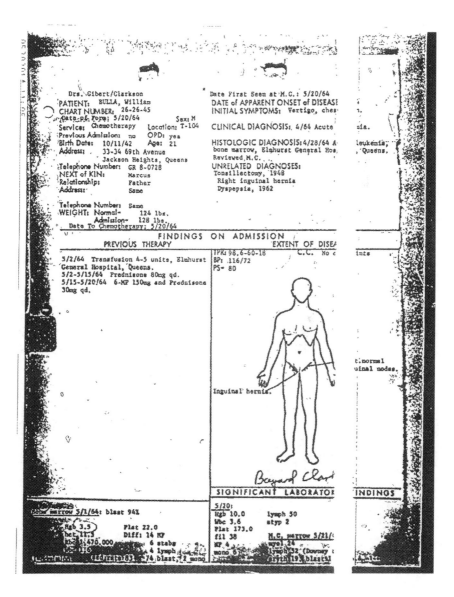

Drs. Gibert/Clarkson

PATIENT: BULLA, William
CHART NUMBER: 26-26-45
Date of Form: 5/20/64
Service: Chemotherapy   Location: T-104   Sex: M
Previous Admission: no   OPD: yes
Birth Date: 10/11/42   Age: 21
Address: 33-34 69th Avenue
         Jackson Heights, Queens
Telephone Number: GR 8-0728
NEXT of KIN: Marcus
Relationship: Father
Address: Same

Telephone Number: Same
WEIGHT: Normal- 124 lbs.
        Admission- 128 lbs.
        Date To Chemotherapy: 5/20/64

Date First Seen at M.C.: 5/20/64
DATE of APPARENT ONSET of DISEASE:
INITIAL SYMPTOMS: Vertigo, ches

CLINICAL DIAGNOSIS: 4/64 Acute   nia.

HISTOLOGIC DIAGNOSIS: 4/28/64 A   leukemia;
bone marrow, Elmhurst General Hos   , Queens,
Reviewed, M.C.
UNRELATED DIAGNOSES:
Tonsillectomy, 1948
 Right inguinal hernia
 Dyspepsia, 1962

FINDINGS ON ADMISSION

PREVIOUS THERAPY   EXTENT OF DISEA

TPR: 98.6-60-18   C.C. No c   ints
5/2/64 Transfusion 4-5 units, Elmhurst   BP: 116/72
General Hospital, Queens.   PS- 80
5/2-5/15/64 Prednisone 80mg qd.
5/15-5/20/64 6-MP 150mg and Prednisone
30mg qd.

Inguinal hernia.   t: normal
                                            uinal nodes.

Bayard Clar

SIGNIFICANT LABORATOR   INDINGS

bone marrow 5/1/64: blast 94%   5/20:
                                      Hgb 10.0   lymph 50
Hgb 3.5   Plat 22.0   Wbc 3.6   atyp 2
hct 11.5   Diff: 14 M?   Plat 173.0
Rbc 1,470,000   6 stabs   fil 38   M.C. marrow 5/21/
Plt 176   4 lymph   M? 4   myel 24
              74 blast 1 mono   mono 6   lymp 32 (Downey t
                                                  lyth 19   blast

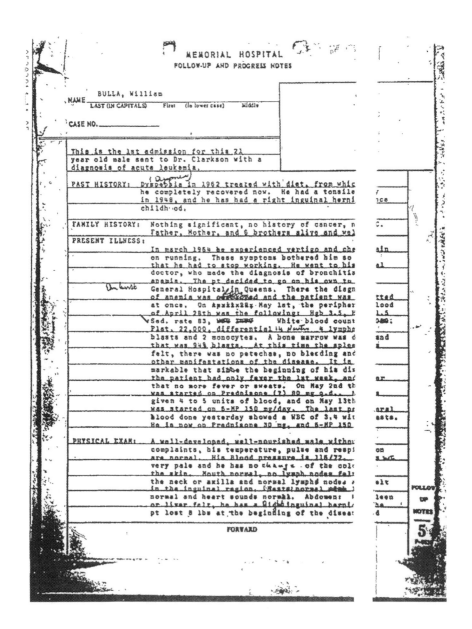

MEMORIAL HOSPITAL
FOLLOW-UP AND PROGRESS NOTES

NAME BULLA, William
      LAST (IN CAPITALS) First (in lower case) Middle

CASE NO.

This is the 1st admission for this 21
year old male sent to Dr. Clarkson with a
diagnosis of acute leukemia.

PAST HISTORY: Dyspepsia in 1962 treated with diet, from whic
               he completely recovered now. He had a tonsile
               in 1948, and he has had a right inguinal herni
               childhood.

FAMILY HISTORY: Nothing significant, no history of cancer, n
                 Father, Mother, and 6 brothers alive and wel

PRESENT ILLNESS:

               In march 1964 he experienced vertigo and che
               on running. These symptoms bothered him so
               that he had to stop working. He went to his
               doctor, who made the diagnosis of bronchitis
               anemia. The pt decided to go on his own to
               General Hospital in Queens. There the diagn
               of anemia was confirmed and the patient was
               at once. On April 28, May 1st, the peripher
               of April 28th was the following: Hgb 3.5, H
               Sed. rate 83,   White blood count
               Plat. 22,000, differential 14 Neutro 4 lymphs
               blasts and 2 monocytes. A bone marrow was d
               that was 94% blasts. At this time the sple
               felt, there was no petechae, no bleeding and
               other manifestations of the disease. It is
               markable that since the beginning of his di
               the patient had only fever the 1st week, and
               that no more fever or sweats. On May 2nd th
               was started on Prednisone (?) 80 mg q.d... i
               given 4 to 5 units of blood, and on May 13th
               was started on 6-MP 150 mg/day. The last pe
               blood done yesterday showed a WBC of 3.4 wit
               He is now on Prednisone 30 mg, and 6-MP 150

PHYSICAL EXAM: A well-developed, well-nourished male withou
                complaints, his temperature, pulse and respi
                are normal. His Blood pressure is 118/72.
                very pale and he has no change of the colo
                the skin. Mouth normal, no lymph nodes fel
                the neck or axilla and normal lymph nodes
                in the inguinal region. Chest: normal
                normal and heart sounds normal. Abdomen:
                or liver felt, he has a right inguinal herni
                pt lost 8 lbs at the beginning of the disea

                          FORWARD

now he is at his normal weight. We discussed th
patient with Dr. Clarkson and decided to do a ne
bone marrow today and while we wait for the result thi
bone marrow and that of the slides done in the b
where he comes from, we decided to keep him on 6-
prednisone as previously. We give him a new app
in one week and at time we will decide what trea
will be done.

Dr. Gibert/lz

MARROW

NAME Bulla William   WARD   DATE 5-21-65   CELL

MYELOID	24.0	PROMYELOCYTES	MYELOCYTES N 3 L J	METAMYELOCYTES N L E
LYMPH.	52.0	Downey types Dukes shift vacuolated		
ERYTHROID	19.4	PRONORMOBLASTS	BASOPHILIC	POLYCHROM. & ORTHOCHROM.
BLASTS	1.0	PLASMA CELLS		RETICULUM CELLS HISTIC
MONOCYTES	4.0	MEGAKAR.	PLATELETS Normal CELLULARITY Acute	CHARACTE

REMARKS:
P.B. Band 6 - Poly 39   Lym 51   mono 4   atypical lymph,

Bulla, William   Adult Chemo   5/28/64
Hgb 9.9   Wbcs 2.3   Weight 127   Temp. 98   Plat. 151.0
        The pt continues to do well on 150 mg daily of 6 M-P an
mg daily of prednisone. He has no symptoms of his disease c
toxicity. On exam there is no adenopathy, purpura, or he   splen-
omegaly. The pt was discussed with Dr. Clarkson and a bone   ow
aspiration was performed. We will continue on 6 M-P and pre   one
as previously and we will see him again in 1 week.

Dr. Meyer/lz

MARROW

NAME Bulla William   WARD silhouette   DATE 5/1/64   CELL

MYELOID	6.0	PROMYELOCYTES	MYELOCYTES N 2 L R	METAMYELOCYTE N L R
LYMPH.	1.0			
ERYTHROID	1.0	PRONORMOBLASTS	BASOPHILIC	POLYCHROM. & ORTHOCHROM.
BLASTS	92.0	PLASMA CELLS		RETICULUM CELLS HISTIC
MONOCYTES		MEGAKAR. Rare	PLATELETS ?	CELLULARITY CHARACTER

REMARKS:
Peripheral blood   Blast 22, myel 2, Poly 10 Lym 64 mono 2 nucleated

NAME_____
LAST (IN CAPITALS)   First   (in lower case)   Middle

CASE NO._____

Bulla, William   Adult Chemo   6-4-64
Hgb 10.4   Wbc 3.6   Weight 128.5   Temp. 97.6
   The pt has been on 150 mg of 6-MP now for 3 weeks and he
on Prednisone current dosage 30 mg for 5 weeks. He remains a
there are no physical findings.
   The pt was discussed with Dr. Clarkson and it was decide
view of the rise in hgb, to discontinue the prednisone while
6-MP. It is also planned to obtain a bone marrow at the pt's
clinic visit in 1 week.
                                        Dr. Savel/lz

6/11/64   Hgb 9.2   Wbc 1.5   Wt. 131 To
Feels fair   Platll 15-7,000
6 MP stopped because of fall in
+ hypocellular marrow Tdy this
8% blast

Return 2 weeks + will aspil marrow + cass
pcttly A Pcbbly call nt
in a week anyong, ccpl thal Cl

NAME Bulla, William   MARROW
                              WARD Chemo   DATE 6/11/64   CELLS C

MYELOID	23.0	PROMYELOCYTES		MYELOCYTES N. 7 E.		METAMYELOCYTES N. 3 B.			100
LYMPHO	30.0								
ERYTHROID	36.0	PRONORMOBLASTS	1	BASOPHILC 2		POLYCHROM & ORTHOCHROM 33			
BLASTS	8.0	PLASMA CELLS		RETICULUM CELLS			RETICULCYT		
PROMYELOCYTES	83.0	MEGAKAR One		PLATELETS Ok		CELLULARITY ↓		CHARACTER M?hf	
		REMARKS							

MARROW

NAME Bulla, William   WARD Adams   DATE 6/25/64

MYELOID	33.5	PROMYELOCYTES		MYELOCYTES N. 2% E. / R. /	METAMYELOCYTES N. 12 E. / B.
LYMPHS.	75				
ERYTHROID	51.0	PRONORMOBLASTS	/	BASOPHILIC 4	POLYCHROM. & ORTHOCHRO 97
BLASTS	4.0	PLASMA CELLS		RETICULUM CELLS	
MONOCYTES	4.0	MEGAKAR OK	PLATELETS OK	CELLULARITY N	CHARAC

REMARKS:

Bulla, Wm   Adult Chemo   6-25-64
Hgb 10.0   Wbc 2.8   Weight 134.5   Temp. 99.4   P
    The pt has been off therapy and he remains asympto
exam the blood pressure is 110/70, the liver was 3 cm b
(Dr. Savel), and was not found by another observer (Dr.
A sternal bone marrow aspiration was performed today w
normal cellularity and a low percentage of blasts (whic
reported later). In view of the normal cellularity it
by Dr. Clarkson, to start ~~pa pt~~ on Mtx 2.5 mg q 8 h and
again in one week.

Bulla, William   Adult Chemo   7-2-
Hgb 10.9   Wbc 2.7 Weight 132.5 Temp. 98.8
    The pt has been on MTX 2.5 mg 3 a day since last wee
and Wbc are normal. Last night he had a rhinitis but toda
normal and has no temperature. Spleen and liver not felt.
discussed with Dr. Clarkson and it was decided to keep the
treatment for one week and to decide next week whether he
admitted to be treated with Mtx and Actin. D (Nitrogen Mus
~~severity~~ of the marrow is normal (as to keep him in remiss:
                         Dr. Gibert/lx

(NAME _____
  LAST (IN CAPITALS)   First (in lower case)   Middle

CASE NO. _____

Bulla, William   ADult Chemo   8-6-64
Hgb 11.5   Wbc 2.8   Weight 134   Temp. 98.6

During the past week the pt has felt well except for _____ ing
nausea wkk with vomiting one occasion. He also had one ep ___ e of
pain on urination, however this subsided spontaneously aft ___ half
hour. He has had no other symptons. Exam today is unrem ___ le. Pt
was discussed with Dr. Clarkson who feels that the 6-MP sh ___ be dsi
continued at this time to gibe the pt a period of rest. h ___ ll return
to Clinic in 1 week at which time further therapy will be ___ ded after
a bone marrow is done.
                              Dr. Williams/lz

Bulla, William   Adult Chemo   8-13-6
Hgb 12.4   WBC 2.5   Weight 132 3/4   Temp. 98.4   . 110.0

Pt has been on no therapy for 1 week and denies any s ___ ss of any
sort except for the onset of a URI 4 days ago which is now ___ iding. Tha ___
nausea and vomiting which he had while on 6- MP has disapp ___ d. At
the present time his physical exam reveals no palpable liv ___ r spleen, no
significant lymph adenopathy, he has some injection of the ___ al pharnxeal
mucus membranes. Discussed with Dr. Krakoff who feels tha ___ view of
his continued border-line thrombocytopenea and leukopenia, ___ pt should
be kept off therapy for 1 more week and return in 1 wk for ___ evaluation
for further therapy.
                              Dr. Williams/lz

Bulla, William   ADult Chemo   8-20-64
Hgb 11.6   Wbc 2.4   WWight 135   Temp. 98.6   Plat. 10

This pt has been off therapy since 8/6/64 and during ___ e time has
been relatively asymptomatic. He reports that he has gai ___ 3 lbs in the
past week, has excellent appetite and now would like to r ___ ck to work if
we think him capable of so doing. Exam today is entirely ___ mal. Discussed
with DR. Krakoff who feels that there is no contraindicat ___ to the pt's
returning to work if he so desires, and that he should be ___ lowed periodically until such time time as he seems to need further t ___ ment. To
return to Clinic in 2 weeks.

                              Dr. Williams/lz

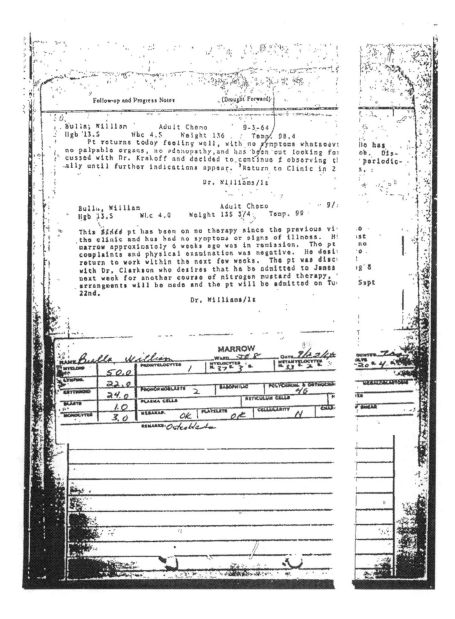

Follow-up and Progress Notes   (Brought Forward)

Bulla, William   Adult Chemo   9-3-64
Hgb 13.5   Wbc 4.5   Weight 136   Temp. 98.4
    Pt returns today feeling well, with no symptoms whatsoev:
no palpable organs, no adenopathy, and has been out looking for
cussed with Dr. Krakoff and decided to continue f observing t
ally until further indications appear. Return to Clinic in 2

                        Dr. Williams/lz

Bulla, William   Adult Chemo   9/:
Hgb 13.5   Wbc 4.0   Weight 135 3/4   Temp. 99

This Sinss pt has been on no therapy since the previous vi
the clinic and has had no symptoms or signs of illness. H
marrow approximately 6 weeks ago was in remission. The pt
complaints and physical examination was negative. He desi
return to work within the next few weeks. The pt was disc
with Dr. Clarkson who desires that he be admitted to James
next week for another course of nitrogen mustard therapy,
arrangements will be made and the pt will be admitted on Tu
22nd.
                        Dr. Williams/lz

MEDICAL ONCOLOGY

1-9-66 Wt 144½ Hgb 11.3 wbc 2.0
Patient is on 100 mg of 6 MP and feeling very well, without any sym
examination is essentially unchanged . . . . no hepatosp
No change in the mucous membranes or skin. Patient is to return in
continue on 100 mg of 6 M. p. d.

Dr. Elser Medical Oncology 1-23-67

MEDICAL ONCOLOGY A

1-23-67 Wt 143½ T 97.4 hgb 13.9 wbc 4.1
Mr. Bulla states that he feels well. He is asymptomatic at this time
works, operated emachine and says the work is easy. Physical examine
pulse 84 and regular, Resp 16, Lungs are clear, Heart - regular rhy
Exam of the abdomen reveals no hepatosplenomegaly. Extremities nega
Mr. Bulla is on 6 MP 100 mg a day. Case discussed with Dr. Clarkson
agreed to continue him on the present medication, and i khrm kati knant
hmm To be seen again in two weeks.

Dr. Zweig Medical Oncology 2-6-67

MEDICAL ONCOLOGY A

2-6-67 Wt 145 T 97.6 hgb 13.8, wbc 2.7, pl 119.0
Pt returns today without any evidence of disease and feels fin
and his pl 119.0, Liver and spleen are not palpable. Case was
Dr. Yu and it was felt that 6 MP should be cut down to 75 mg d
the patient should return in one week . Inasmuch as he is near
course of 6 MP , it was felt that a bone marrow should be def
week or two until the end of the course. Patient will return i

Dr. Guild Medical Oncology 2-1

2/13/67 Wt 147½ T 97⁴ Hgb 14.4 WBC 3.0
PS. 10.

Pt completely asymptomatic.
PE Heart & lungs clear. No pulp. of
no nodes.

Sternal marrow aspirated today.

D.C. 6MP today.
Return 1 wk for act. D.

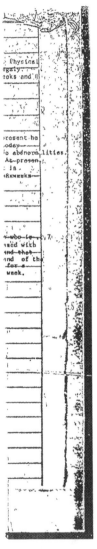

MEMORIAL HOSPITAL
FOLLOW-UP AND PROGRESS NOTES

NAME _Bulla, William_
LAST (IN CAPITALS)   First (in lower case)   Middle

CASE NO. _26-26-45_

BULLA, William   ADULT CHEMOTHERAPY   March 29, 1965

Patient was just discharged from Ewing 8 on Saturday evening hav   eceived .2 mg.
per kg. nitrogen mustard on Saturday afternoon followed by occa   l nausea and
vomiting but has not had any nausea since. His WBC is 2.3 today   ysical examination is completely negative. He was advised to return to clini   rsday but
stated it would be inconvenient therefore he will come to clinic   onday. He was
told if he has any symptoms of cold or sore throat in terms of a   ulocytic angina
he should call me or Dr. Clarkson. We will see him Monday in on   k.

gcl   Martin Weiner,

BULLA, William   ADULT CHEMOTHERAPY   April 5, 1965

Patient feels fine. There are no particular complaints. His phy   findings are
negative and he does not have any particular complications due to   toxicity. He
still holds WBC of 2.4 since the time of his nitrogen mustard on   '65. Patient
was discussed with Dr. Clarkson and according to rotating (cyclic)   e of treatment
he is due to start on Methotrexate and he will be placed on 5 mg./   and will be
seen in one week.

gcl   Stojan Solaric   D. SS/b1

BULLA, William   ADULT CHEMOTHERAPY   pril 12, 1965

Patient started last week on Methotrexate, 5 mg./day. He has no   oms of toxicity and his blood count is good. Patient was discussed with Dr.   kson and it
was decided to keep him on same dose of Methotrexate, 5 mg./day,   e will be seen
in ten days when a new bone marrow will be done.

gcl   Pierre Gibert,   PG/b1

4/22/65   Hgb 12.1   WBC 4.2   Wt 137   T 92°   L Ro

Nausea + vomiting, today marr

hypocellular + megaloblastic N. bl

Stop MTX for 2 weeks only!

Return 2 weeks.   CC

FORWARD.

HEMATOLOGY
11-29-71 Wt 67.5 kg T 97 wbc 4.7 hgb 15, pl 175.0

Mr. Bulla is a long term ALL survivor who is being maintained on
of 6 MP, Actinomycin, Thio TEPA and Methotrexate. He is presently
of the third week of Methotrexate portion.

He is completely asymptomatic and on physical exam, no abnormalit
Bone marrow taken last week showed 60% myeloids, 25 % erythroids
megakaryocytes and a normal cellularity.

Disposition: Will continue on the Methotrexate for the next two w
he will return to clinic. His case was discussed with Dr. Clarkso:

                                    Dr. Turner Hematology 1

HEMATOLOGY
12-13-71 Wt 67.5 kg T 99 hgb 15.3 wbc 3.3 pl 119.0 BP 110/70
This is a 29 year old white male who is a long term survivor
being maintained on an old protocol. His last marrow on Nov 1!
remission. For the past two weeks the patient has been taking
for 4 days a week. He has been completely asymptomatic without
Exam, reveals a husky wt man in no distress. Mouth and pharynx
is papillated. There is no adenopathy. Chest is clear. Heart r
without gallops. There are no abdominal masses or organomegaly
edema.

COMMENT: The patient was discussed with Dr. D owling. He will c
for the next two weeks on the same schedule as previously and

                                    Dr. Idhe Hematology 12-27-

---

HEMATOLOGY
12-27-71 Wt 67 kg T 97.6 hgb 15.0 wbc 3.6 pl 148.0 BP 130/7
Mr. Bulla continues to do well with no complaints.
Physical examination: There is no evidence of disease. Pati
on the Methotrexate 5 mg four days out of seven and return i
time we should have a marrow and institution of Thio TEPA.

                                    Dr. Gee Hematology 1-10-7

[right column fragments:]
ring schedule
ne beginning

re detected
2% blasts, no

t which time

i

bb currently
ined in
of Methotrexate
s or purpura,
benign. ngua
is regular
re is no

e Methotrexate
 to clinic then.

to continue
weeks, at which

Follow-up and Progress Notes   (Brought Forward)

HEMATOLOGY SERVICE   MARROW DIFFERENTIAL   EXAMINED BY

NAME *Bulla William* # 26-26-45   WARD OPD   DATE 10/9/74   CELLS C: D 200

MYELOID	52.5 %	PROMYELOCYTES #	MYELOCYTES N. B.	METAMYELOCYTES 2 N. B.	POL N.
LYMPHS.	11.5	PLASMA CELLS	HISTIOCYTES		RETICULUM CELLS	POL
ERYTHROID	23.5	PRONORMOBLASTS	BASOPHILIC	POLYCHROM. 8 ORTHOCHROM. 47	
BLASTS	1.0	MEGAKARYOCYTES see mn	PLATELETS	CELLULARITY mod.-mk √	CHARACTER OF's
MONOCYTES	4.5	REMARKS:			
PLASMA					

HEMATOLOGY
November 11, 1974   WBC 3.6, HGB 13.6, PLAT 128,0
Mr. Bulla is a 32 yr old man who had ALL diagnosed about 1 1 yrs ago. He
off chemotherapy for 6 months. He feels well and has no complaints. On ph
examination there is no evidence of disease. Bone marrow aspirate perform
sternum without difficulty. Pt wishes to have circumcisionand at Dr. Dow]
a private appointment is being made for him with Dr. Whitmore.

PLAN: RTC in 2 months for repeat bone marrow.
                                                      Dr. E.

HEMATOLOGY SERVICE 5   MARROW DIFFERENTIAL   EXAMINED B

NAME *Bulla. William* # 26-26-45   WARD OPD   DATE 11/11/74 CELLS

MYELOID	%	PROMYELOCYTES #	MYELOCYTES N. B.	METAMYELOCYTES N. B.	
LYMPHS		PLASMA CELLS	HISTIOCYTES		RETICULUM CELLS
ERYTHROID		PRONORMOBLASTS	BASOPHILIC	POLYCHROM & ORTHOCHROM	
BLASTS		MEGAKARYOCYTES	PLATELETS	CELLULARITY	CHARACTER OF
MONOCYTES		REMARKS:			
PLASMA					

BULLA, Wil

DATE _____

26-26-45

Record patient

zero number

HEMATOLOGY

3-10-75 Wt. 68: BP 116/64: T. 36.5: P 80: WBC 4.3: Hgb. 14.0: PLT 126   - little

He had a few episodes of nosebleeding after sneezing - not really blee
streaks of blood. Thisis probably due to a local lesion.

P.E.   Entirely unremarkable.

PLAN: Bone marrow aspiration performed sternally without difficulty
        RTC in one month.

                                                Dr. Reich/dm

HEMATOLOGY SERVICE ST   MARROW DIFFERENTIAL   EXAMINE   OTH

NAME Bulla, William # 26-26-45 WARD MD DATE 3/10/75 CEL   UNTED 240

MYELOID	48.0 %	PROMYELOCYTES 1	MYELOCYTES N. 6 E. a.	METAMYELOCYTES N. 20 E. 3 a.	1 &2 a.
LYMPHS	19.0	PLASMA CELLS 2	HISTIOCYTES		RETICULUM CELLS	IRRON & TOPHILIA
ERYTHROID	27.0	PRONORMOBLASTS	BASOPHILIC 1	POLYCHROM & OXYHROMOBL 52	ILOBLASTOSIS
BLASTS	2.0	MEGAKARYOCYTES 1	PLATELETS	CELLULARITY cell. mod	CHARACTE		AM
MONOCYTES	30	REMARKS:			
PLASMA	1.0				

HEMATOLOGY

April 7, 1975   WBC 4.8, HGB 14.5, PLAT 159.0

Mr. Bulla is a 32 yr old man with ALL who has now been off therapy for   nths
having been on therapy for approximately 10 yrs. He feels well and has   mplaints
PE shows no evidence of disease.

PLAN: No therapy today. RTC in 1 month for bone marrow.

                                                Dr. Phil

                        FORWARD

HEMATOLOGY
May 5, 1975   WBC 4.5 HGB 13.3, PLAT 162.0

Mr Bulla is a 32 yr old man with ALL now off all chemotherapy and   g well.
He has no complaints and pe is NED.
Bone marrow aspirate performed from the sternum without difficult
RTC in 1 month.

HEMATOLOGY SERVICE St   **MARROW DIFFERENTIAL**   Dr. Phillips   of Phi

NAME	Bulla. William	# 26-26-45	WARD	10	DATE	5/5/75	s COUNTED	200

		PROMYELOCYTES	1	MYELOCYTES	10.2	METAMYELOCYTES	17.1	POLYS	74.2
MYELOID	54.0%					RETICULUM C:			
LYMPHS.	18.0	PLASMA CELLS	HISTIOCYTES			POLYCHROMATOPHILIA			
ERYTHROID	24.0	NORMOBLASTS	BASOPHILIC		POLYCHROM. & ORTHOCH 47				
BLASTS	2.0	MEGAKARYOCYTES (not seen) PLATELETS (adequate)	CELLULARITY						
MONOCYTES	2.0	REMARKS:							
PLASMA									

HEMATOLOGY
June 2, 1975   WBC 5.2, HGB 13.3, PLAT 162.0
Mr Bulla is a 32 yrold man with ALL diagnosed 11 yrs ago, who   chemotherapy
for 10 yrs and has now been off all drugs for 13 months. He fee   nerally very well.
He noticed that he has some stuffiness of his nose from the al   itinner at work
He also has been complaining of occasional groin rash. PE is NI

PLAN: Mycostatin topical powder PRN.
        RTC in 1 month.
                                                              D: llips

BULLA, Willi
26-26-45

DATE _____

5 January 1976: NEUROLOGY CLINIC VISIT

This 32 y/o man has had ALL for 11 years.in remission and off medicat   ince 1974.
He is referred at the present time because on the 29th of December he   lained to
Dr. Dowling of 3 weeks of pressure in the head along with bilateral m   ary pain.
He also complained of visual problems but apparently these are of lon   ding and
he has not sought ophthalmologic advice. Dr. Dowling tapped him, dis   d a pressure
of 283; a cell count is not present in the chart but there were appar   no
malignant cells. Protein was 10 but the glucose was 32. At the pres   me the
patient says his headache is pretty well gone and he feels much bette   ether
this cleared before or after the spinal tap is not clear. He states   has been
no substantial change in his vision over the last several years altho   does
have some difficulty with vision which he cannot further describe. H   no other
complaints.

ON EXAMINATION a language barrier makes history and mental status tes   ifficult
but his mental state appears to be normal. The optic fundi show disc   rather
large cups which do not appear unusually deep but which move the vesse   mewhat
to the sides. There is, however, no evidence of papilledema and the   ature
looks normal. The remainder of the neurological examination including   exes
are intact.

IMPRESSION: In view of the abnormal spinal tap this needs a rep   make
certain that this is not the beginning of meningeal   emia.
He also needs and ophthalmological examination which I have told him   es not
want a repeat spinal tap now but will return for a bone marrow next Mo   and will
come up here next Monday at 1 P.M. when I will tap him.

Jerome B. Posner, M.D./sb

1/iv Seen today - Bill feels much better &
he complains of some impotency since
spinal tap. - his headache lida cleare
P̄ - unremarkable
Marrow is done -
He will be seen for repeat tap c̄
today as above

FORWARD

FOLLOW
UP
NOTES

5

P-8625

NAME BULLA WILLIAM # 26-26-45				WARD OPD	DATE 1/12/76	CELL	NTED 100	
MYELOID	60.0%	PROMYELOCYTES		MYELOCYTES		METAMYELOCYTES N 3 E 8		
LYMPHS.	2.0	PLASMA CELLS	HISTIOCYTES				RETICULUM CELLS	
ERYTHROID	13.0	PRONORMOBLASTS		BASOPHILIC		POLYCHROM & ORTHOCHROM		
BLASTS		MEGAKARYOCYTES rare seen	PLATELETS		CELLULARITY M/C	CHARACTER	
MONOCYTES	1.0	REMARKS:						
PLASMA								

He is now asymptomatic but because of the abnormal findings on the last lumbar puncture that tap is repeated. The opening ___ 152, and 10 cc of crystal clear fluid were removed and sent to the lab cytology, protein, glucose and protein electrophoresis. The closing pr___ 110. The procedure was done without difficulty. Since he is asymptoma___ be sent home to await the lab results, which I suspect will be normal.

Jerome B. Posner, M.D./cd

HEMATOLOGY: 2/5/76

Pt with ALL in remission for a number of yrs. He is off therapy now for ___ 2 yrs and doing well. Most recently he had a headache and workup includ___ cytology of which is negative and protein which is normal. He has no oth___ On examination, PS 100%, W 69.5 kg., BP 110/78, T 36., P 80, regular. W___ HGB 13.7, PLAT 156. There is no adenopathy. Lungs are clear. No viscero___ Normal mental status, normal cranial nerves.

PLAN: Continue off therapy and observe monthly. Pt will have a marrow ___ from now.

Dr. Hay___

3/8/76 No complaints
Cts good
Pt ⊖
BM done
RTC 1 month

F. Plenbaur

NAME _____ BULLA, William _____ ROOM NO. _____
    LAST (IN CAPITALS)   First   (in lower case or script)   Middle   FLOOR ___ J
154.1   CASE NO. ___ 26 26 45 ___ CL. SERV. _

NATURE OF OPERATION ___ Right inguinal herniorrhaphy

ATTENDING SURGEON Dr. ___ McPeak _____ DATE OF OPERATION _____

OPER. SURG. Dr. ___ Lee/McPeak ____ 1st Ass't Dr. ___ Pang ____ 2nd Ass't Dr. ___

ANESTHETIST _____ KIND OF ANESTHESIA _____

DIAG. PRE-OP. ___ Right inguinal hernia, indirect DIAG. POST-OP. _____

DICTATED BY DR. ___ Lee/jt-3/19/73 _____ DATE DICTATED _____

DESCRIBE: (1) OPERATIVE FINDINGS and (2) OPERATIVE TECHNIQUE. Keep notes under each and relevant. Limit OPERATIVE FINDINGS to a description of facts revealed at operation. Do not include former diseases could not be observed during the operation simply say so and go on to a description of the operative technique, of operative findings under OPERATIVE TECHNIQUE

FINDINGS: There was a typical indirect inguinal hernia with
    sac which was reaching the upper portion of the ac
The inguinal floor itself felt normal as examined from within
was no femoral hernia noted.

PROCEDURE: With the patient under general anesthesia in the
    position, the entire abdomen, groins, scrotum and
thighs were prepared and draped in routine manner. A semitre
incision along the skin crease toward the pubic tubercle was
and after ligating a few bleeders with 000 chromic catgut, th
ternal oblique aponeurosis was opened to the external ring,
nerves were identified, and these were protected throughout t
cedure. At this point the spermatic cord structures were iso
at the pubic tubercle and the hernial sac isolated. The sac
separated from the cord structures and the distal portion com
freed. With a finger inside the sac, the rest of the cord at
were dissected off the sac to the level of the internal ring.
this was completed and after being sure that nothing was caug
the proximal portion of the hernial sac, a transfixing suture
000 black silk was placed to the highest portion of the herni
and this was ligated and another one put just distal to the f
The sac was then excised. The internal ring was then reconst
by bringing the transversalis fascia down to the anterior fem
sheath and medially. Medially this was continued in a fashio

9

RECORD OF OPERATION

(continued from obverse)

imbricate the whole floor, using the upper portion of the tr   rsalis
fascia down to the iliopubic tract. This seemed to be very s   ng.
and a good piece of tissue; and the reconstructed floor felt
The umbilical tape from around the cord was removed and the   om
placed back into its normal position, and this was pulled do   ted
the scrotum. The external oblique aponeurosis was then appr   ain
with interrupted 000 black silk, and after placing about thr   h
catgut sutures for Scarpa's fascia, the skin was approximate
interrupted 0000 nylon stitches.

The patient withstood the whole procedure well and was taken   the
recovery room in good condition.

MEMORIAL HOSPITAL   3 19 73

SURGICAL PATHOLOGY

SUBMITTED
BY DOCTOR
SUBMITTED SLIDES ☐   SUBMITTED BLOCKS ☐

OUTSIDE
SOURCE

BULLA,
30   26
GASTRIC

LIAN
45

PATIENT NAME AND ADDRESS

LABORATORY USE ONLY
☐ SMALL BIOPSY   ☐ SPECIMEN   ☐ SMEARS   ☐ CLOT   ☐ IMMEDIATE
EXAM (F S)

1. Spc ® hernia   4   7
   sac

2   5   8

3   6   9

ANATOMIC SOURCE
OF SPECIMEN

CLINICAL
DIAGNOSIS

PREVIOUS ACCESSIONS IN
THIS LABORATORY   ☐ YES   ☐ NO   PREVIOUS PATHOLOGY
                                      NUMBERS

SIGNIFICANT CLINICAL DATA (USE ANATOMIC STAMPS WHEN POSSIBLE)   AGE   SEX

DISPOSITION OF REPORT IF
OTHER THAN TO CHART

PATHOLOGY REPORT
(SEE REVERSE SIDE FOR GROSS PATHOLOGY)

ACCESSION DATE
19 MR

AREA
33144

DATE OF
REPORT   3-21-73

MICROSCOPIC REPORT BY DR. P. Rosen/pb

#1. Hernia sac.

CHART COPY

MEMORIAL HOSPITAL

DISCHARGE SUMMARY

Date   March 26, 1973

BULLA WILLIA[

26 26 45

James Ewing P   on
Memorial Hosp

DATE OF ADMISSION: 3/18/73

DATE OF DISCHARGE: 3/24/73

ADMISSION DIAGNOSIS: Right indirect inguinal hernia
                            Acute lymphocytic leukemia in remi:

SUMMARY OF MANAGEMENT: This 30 year old male with known
                            lymphocytic leukemia in remission i
9 years has had a hernia in the right groin. Patient claims that he ha
this hernia for over 20 years and recently became somewhat larger and m
painful. His leukemia has been regularly followed by the oncology grou;
and has been in satisfactory remission for a long time.

PHYSICAL EXAMINATION: Well developed, well nourished mal
                            with a medium size indirect inguin
hernia on the right side with none on the opposite side. Both testicle
somewhat atrophic but the rest of the physical examination was unremark

                            Routine laboratory examinations in ng,
                            CBC, urinalysis, screening profile   G,
chest x-rays all within normal limits. On March 19, 1973, right inguin
hernia was repaired and patient had a medium size indirect hernia with   y
good inguinal floor. Postoperatively, the patient did well and was dis ed
March 24th to be seen in the clinic in a few days.

                            Patient was also seen by the hemat
group for his leukemia during this hospitalization and he will also be
an appointment for both clinics.

FINAL DIAGNOSIS: Right indirect inguinal hernia

Dictated by Dr. Lee
3/24/73

DISCH.
SUMM.
1B

DISCHARGE SUMMARY

Admission Diagnoses (include previous diagnoses):

Acute leukemia

Patient:	BULLA, Willia.
Chart No.:	26-26-45
Adm. Date:	7/14/64
Disch. Date:	7/16/64
Location:	JE8
Attending:	Dr. B. Cla

Discharge Diagnoses:
Acute leukemia

Consultations: none

Condition on Discharge:

Prognosis: guarded

Disposition: Chemothera; nic

Histologic Diagnosis: 4/28/64 Acute leukemia, bone marrow, reviewed M.C.

Discharge Medications:
none

Surgical Procedure (if any):
none

See admission CS1 form for documentation of disease, previous therapy, pı (story and unrelated diagnoses, and findings on admission.

Course in Hospital:

This is a 21 year old white man who has acute leukemia in remission and admitted to receive actinomycin D and nitrogen mustard as part of a stud the use of these two drugs in leukemia in remission. On 7/14/64 he rece actinomycin D 1mg i.v. and nitrogen mustard 11.6mg i.v., without complic. He was discharged on 7/16/64, to be followed in the chemotherapy clinic.

J. Williams, M.D./

DISCHARGE SUMMARY

Admission Diagnoses (include previous diagnoses):
Acute leukemia in remission.

Patient: BULLA, William
Chart No.: 26-26-45
Adm. Date: 9/22/64
Disch. Date: 9/23/64
Location: JE8
Attending: Dr. B. Cla

Discharge Diagnoses:

Acute leukemia in remission.

Consultations: none.

Condition on Discharge:

Prognosis: guarded

Disposition: Chemotherapy

Histologic Diagnosis:
4/28/64 Acute leukemia, bone marrow,
reviewed at M.C.
Surgical Procedure (if any):
None.

Discharge Medications:
None.

See CS1 form (attached) for documentation of disease, previous therapy, ps   story,
and findings on admission.
Course in Hospital:
This patient was admitted as a part of a study of acute leukemia in remiss   to
receive nitrogen mustard. On the evening of 9/22/64 he was given nitrogen   rd
25mg (0.4mg/Kg). He was discharged the following day to be followed in Ch   erapy
Clinic.

Jeanine Williams, M.D. / egm

THERAPY

9/29/64 Nitrogen Mustard 0.4mg/Kg (25mg) i.v.

COMPLICATIONS

None

X-RAYS (No,)

None

SPECIAL STUDIES

Study of acute leuk .n
remission.

LABORATORY FINDINGS

Hgb 12.2
Hct 36
Wbc 4.4
Plat 187.0
Fils 56, NF 3, eo 1, mono 10, lymphs 30.

PS: 100 PHYSICAL FINDIN
Weight 58.5Kg
TPR: 98.6-88-20
BP: 124/64

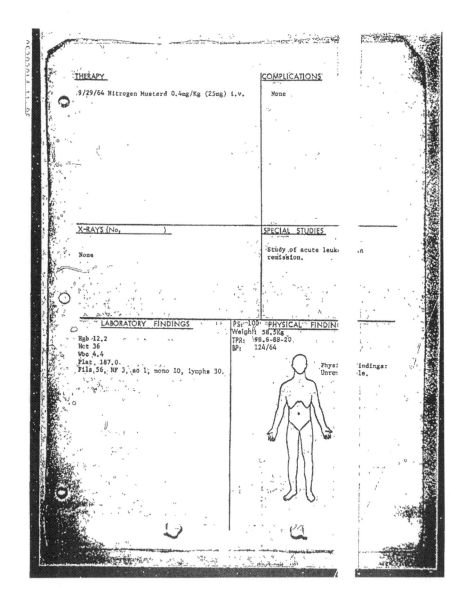

Phys indings:
Unre le.

DISCHARGE SUMMARY

Admission Diagnoses (include previous diagnoses):
Acute leukemia in remission.

Patient: BULLA, Willis
Chart No.: 26-26-45
Adm. Date: 11/13/6（
Disch. Date: 11/14/6（
Location: JEB   je: 21.
Attending: Dr. B. （   on

Discharge Diagnoses:
Acute leukemia in remission.

Consultations: None

Condition on Discharge: d

Prognosis: guarded

Disposition: Chemothe: :linic

Histologic Diagnosis: 4/28/64 Acute leukemia,
bone marrow, reviewed at M.C.

Discharge Medications:
None

Surgical Procedure (if any):
None

See admission CS1 form (attached) for documentation of disease, prev   therapy,
past history and findings on admission.

Course in Hospital:
This patient was admitted as a part of a study of acute leukemia in   sion,
to receive actinomycin D 1mg given intravenously on the evening of a   ion.
He experienced a slight hypotensive episode following Demerol and M   al
but there was no residual to this and he was discharged on the follo   day
to be followed in Chemotherapy Clinic.

Carlton A. MacDonald
Dr. Carlton A. MacDonald / egm

Carlton C. MacDonald

THERAPY	COMPLICATIONS & OTHER	NGS
11/13/64 Actinomycin D 1mg i.v.	Slight transient hypote	

X-RAYS (No.)	SPECIAL STUDIES
None	Study of acute leukemi. remission.

LABORATORY FINDINGS	PS: 100 PHYSICAL FINDINGS	
Hgb 12.3	Weight: not recorded	
Wbc 2.5	TPR: 98-80-20	
Plat 200.0	BP: 115/70	
Urine: negative		Physical ex tion: Unremarkab

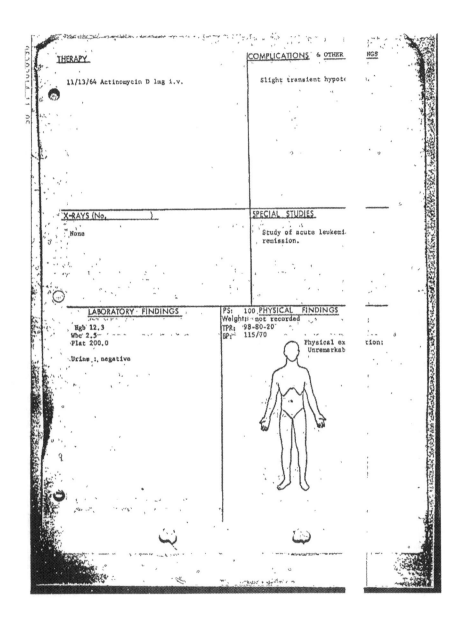

DISCHARGE SUMMARY

Admission Diagnoses (include previous diagnoses):

Acute leukemia in remission.

Coded

Discharge Diagnoses:

Acute leukemia in remission.

Histologic Diagnosis: 4/28/64 Acute leukemia.
bone marrow. Reviewed at M.C.

Surgical Procedure (if any):
None.

Patient: BULLA, Will
Chart No.: 26-26-
Adm. Date: 3/26/6?
Disch. Date: 3/27/6?
Location: JE8   Age: 22
Attending: Dr. B. C   n

Consultations: none

Condition on Discharge   good

Prognosis: guarded

Disposition: Chemothe   Clinic

Discharge Medication
None

See admission CS1 form for documentation of disease, previous therapy,   history
and findings on admission.
Course in Hospital:
This patient was admitted as part of a study of acute leukemia in remi   to
receive nitrogen mustard intravenously. The patient's white count on   sion
was 2.3, and the following morning he was given 0.2mg/Kg (12mg) of nit   mustard
intravenously with minimal side effects. He was discharged to be fol   in clinic.

R.S. Martin, M.D. / egn

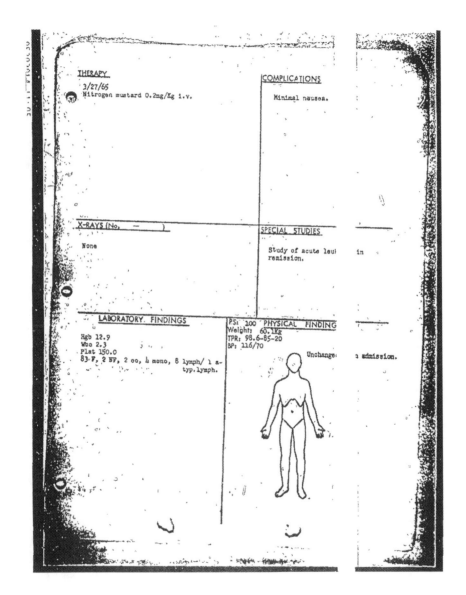

THERAPY

3/27/65
Nitrogen mustard 0.2mg/Kg i.v.

COMPLICATIONS

Minimal nausea.

X-RAYS (No. —)

None

SPECIAL STUDIES

Study of acute leu in
remission.

LABORATORY FINDINGS

Hgb 12.9
Wbc 2.3
Plat 150.0
83 F, 2 BF, 2 oo, 4 mono, 8 lymph/ 1 a-
                                typ. lymph.

PS: 100   PHYSICAL FINDING
Weight: 60.1Kg
TPR: 98.6-85-20
BP: 116/70

Unchange admission.

THERAPY

7/14/64 Actinomycin D 1mg i.v.
         HN2   11.6mg i.v.

COMPLICATIONS

X-RAYS (No. 195-245)

7/15/64 Chest: WNL

SPECIAL STUDIES

LABORATORY FINDINGS

7/15/64
Hgb 12.0
hct 34
Wbc 4.1
Plat 203.0
retic 2.3

Urine: unremarkable

BUN 11
FBS 90
BSP 5
uric ac 7.0
remainder of LFT: WNL

PHYSICAL FINDINGS

P:100; Weight: 57.3
TPR: 98.6-60-16
BP: 100/80

normal physical findings.

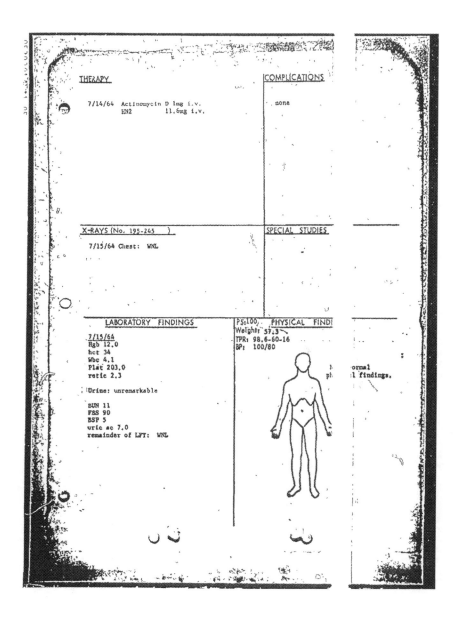

Appendix

I hereby am appending a selection of major personal chronological records encompassing positive and negative passage results which occurred during the period of my life covering a span of close to 4 decades beginning back in the summer of year 1975, precisely, at the time when my chemo research program indefinitely became discontinued. Henceforth, I was blessed, remaining in a stage of remission, and successfully continuing free from taking any medication, still unto present year 2014. It exactly has been 39 long years since destiny had it written that I had to survive in order to carry an important mission in this confused unsubordinated society in which we coexist. I have been blessed by Almighty God, most of all for keeping me alive in this complicated world of ours. It is noteworthy to mention, that as far as Memorial Sloan Kettering Cancer Center is technically concerned, I was never officially declared completely cured, although free from cancerous lymphoma symptoms. However, taking into consideration the facts recorded after miraculously following an extensive trajectory protocol associated with a Chemotherapy Research program over more than an eleven year period, the result was to discontinue my involvement in the research program.

Year 1975 was marred by a series of events culminating in a historical one of epic proportion, when my chemotherapy treatment reached the zenith, right after undergoing an intensive voluntary cancer research program at Memorial Sloan Kettering Cancer Center in Manhattan, New York, USA.

Year 1975, during early winter season, after a long complicated agonizing illness, my father finally passed away while succumbing to the disease, resting in peace. He was still relatively young at 73 years of age considering his family tree's historic data. A typical case was my Aunt Rita, who passed away shortly after celebrating her last birthday at the age of 106 years old. She was modest revealing her longevity's secret, and quote: "First, do not let stress rule your life; second, do not ever get married." Hmm! Quite frankly the last one is a bit difficult to apply indeed.

Four years later in May of Year 1979, I fully accomplished a memorable personal long-term goal, a 3 day bike-a-thon covering a total of 254 miles round trip from the city of Great Neck, Long Island, New York across Montauk Point, the furthermost distance point on Eastern Long Island, New York. The mission's objective was the America Cancer Society fundraiser for which my total contribution was over $300.

At the beginning of fall season in September of Year 1979, together with great enthusiastic support from a small group of avid tennis players, I finally turned founding a Tennis organization into reality, which I called WB Sport international. As time passed by, I successfully expanded from the original 6 registered members to 127 very active registered members, as well as voluntary substitute players.

The Year 1980 will always be remembered by a series of family sequences of success, and tragic events. During the Fourth of July National Independence Day celebration, family relatives and friends received the ominous news from a hospital somewhere north in the State of California that my youngest brother Joseph, and Alba his wife, suffered a dreadful car accident and she instantly died at the scene of accident. She perished so tragically at such a tender age of 20 years old, precisely on her birthday celebration, a painful unimaginable scenario.

Late October of Year 1980, following a rigorous consistent training preparation for the world's prestigious New York City running marathon, Clemencia's dreams finally became reality while participating and successfully setting a best personal record time of 3 hours, and 51 minutes. It was a day to reckon with; so much collective excitement shared by all those of us who congregated to cheer her as she crossed the finish line!

Later that week after the marathon was history, Clemencia and I were returning from Paradise Island, Bahamas, after a well-deserved and relaxing vacation. Upon arriving at La Guardia Airport, Queens, New York, we received information that Paul Paolino's (Ingrid's fiance') sister Stacey had passed away at the young age of 27 years; she was having some serious, complicated health issues. The following day, the Church service was a very touching emotional scene, especially watching all of the youngest students from her elementary class among mourners, participating abreast with all of those there present in orderly procession, sad indeed.

Year 1982 Clemencia once again decided to participate for the second time in the New York City Marathon. Everything was going well on her training schedule. Alas! The unexpected occurred during the Memorial Day Holiday at the end of May. While traveling together with another couple, Jaime and Gloria Camargo, friends of ours, all of a sudden we became involved in a car accident. Unfortunately she suffered serious lacerations on both knees, which kept her away from training; thus after serious contemplation she disqualified herself from running in the prestigious N.Y. C. Marathon race.

October of Year 1982, the day of the race finally arrived and Clemencia obviously was determined to run the race against all odds without any hesitation, in spite of the fact that she still was experiencing some issues. Somehow, for her own sake, I did voluntarily choose to join her at the race course at the last half stage. The rest was history; I joined her by the 15th mile distance, and kept abreast with her until the 25th mile distance lap. What a colossal experience I had, living moments of glory, spectators cheering me on and receiving encouraging complements of "how good physically" I was looking. Ha! Ha! She proudly finished in a combined 4 hours and 21 minutes time. According to the official weather report, it was the warmest New York marathon race ever registered.

Summer of 1983, I enthusiastically registered to participate in the prestigious Pepsi Cola Annual Invitational Bike-a-thon, held in Central Park over 24 hours in a 6 mile closed circuit loop in Manhattan, New York. I successfully accomplished my personal best covering a total of 389 miles with 7 interval hours of rest. The winner's distance record was over 850 miles; some achievement, huh?

During the year 1986-1987, Ingrid reached the zenith of her college tennis career by winning the Metropolitan College Invitational at Flushing Tennis Center stadium, Queens, New York. She was selected as the number one Athlete of the Year for her personal achievements, setting an all-time record of 48 wins and 5 defeats during her years representing Queens College, thus winning the highest honor given to the best athlete of the year: The Silver Knight Award. With faith and perseverance, she did accomplish her goal, thus fulfilling my childhood dreams, The Lord bless her now and forever, Amen.

Year 1987 became a memorable epoch, when Ingrid and Paul officially celebrated their wedding ceremony with their four grandmothers present, family, relatives, and friends, as well. They solemnly tied the knot at Kings Point Military Academy Chapel, surrounded by gorgeous grounds, and a bit later followed by a fabulous reception at the Lieutenant's Club Hall overlooking the East river, the borough of Manhattan's spectacular background scenery. An unforgettable date in my life's anal.

Spring of 1988, I really was encouraged by relatives and friends to register and join them as a participant in the Newsday Annual Half Marathon, at Eisenhower Park Nassau, Long Island, New York. I obviously felt so well fit, attributed to excellent training and rigorous preparation. What ensued next? Very positive personal results! I finished the race without incident, and only hours later, immediately after the party ceremony had concluded, I was on the tennis courts playing, enjoying the camaraderie, and having fun.

Summer of 1989, during the prestigious Great Neck Annual Tennis Open Tournament, WB Sport International had a great deal of pride when one of our lovely members, Claudine Moschella, graciously accepted the challenge by participating in the tournament. She went as far reaching semifinals in the Woman's Open Division. Claudia, you always will be remembered not only for your talent, and sportsmanship, but your terrific personality, as well!

On November 15, 1992, I practically was stunned with a fantastic birthday surprise party, celebrating my 50 years of age. It is hard to believe, but only through a celestial miracle have I reached this plateau of my existence. There are moments of solitude when I find in spiritual reflection, that I arrive to true realization, and humbly prostate on my knees, I express my most profound gratitude to my Lord's merciful intervention and blessings bestowed upon my soul. His planned mission imposed unto myself on Earth made it possible for these jubilees.

August 15, 1993, their first offspring is born to Ingrid and Paul, thus officially becoming parents to a baby girl named Lauren Clemencia. And to my wife and I, our adorable first grandchild, a wonderful blessing gift from Almighty God. The start of a new generation, Amen!

July 20, 1996, almost four years later, their second offspring is born to Ingrid and Paul. Very proud parents of a baby boy named Paul John, he became our second grandchild, a real bundle of love, a wonderful gift blessing from Almighty God.

On August 29 1996, I practically was confronted with one of the most difficult personal decisions I have ever made since I left my native city of Bogota, Colombia, back on January 20, 1959. Now with a great deal of mixed emotions, and wonderful memories, I finally am leaving behind my dear mother, brothers, and friends, to be reunited with my family in the city of Boca Raton, Florida, U.S.A. It has been almost four years since Ingrid, Paul, and Lauren established permanent residence there, then Clemencia a year later. Therefore, I stayed behind with no other alternative but living three years by myself. I used to kid around by saying and I quote, "they were perhaps, my life's best years." Ha! Ha!

October 19, 1996, almost 2 months after I permanently had moved to Boca Raton, my beloved mother "sumerced," finally had her wishes come true when she quickly passed away at 87 years of age, and the angels took her away to Paradise. I shall always remember her as the most beautiful woman that ever walked on the face of the Earth. Her life in this World was characteristic of a typical innocent helpless victim who in the name of the Lord accepted with resignation the horrendous social injustice that has prevailed throughout hundreds of generations. As long as I live I shall never forget the unforgiving vicious existence and suffering she endured while still alive in this World.

April 29,1997, with a great deal of sadness, after 17 years of successful operation W.B. Sport International almost entirely collapsed, thus leaving us with no other alternative but to permanently suspend any further activities. Wonderful times, and unforgettable memories we all had, I must say indeed. My kudos to Joan Morsan whose personal dedication, and clerical and artistic advertising expertise, kept our member under the umbrella for a period of 17 years, awesome to say the least.

3 years later on May 25, 1999, Ingrid and Paul were blessed once again for a third time, becoming very proud parents to fraternal twin baby boys. Jon Michael first was born, and following right after a 27 minute interval, Steven Andrew was born. It turned out to be of unprecedented historical magnitude, since they became the first twins born among the Paolino's or Bulla's family trees.

For two consecutive years, in the summers of 2001 and 2002, I reached the zenith of my athletic ability in a competitive series marked by self-imposed physical heroic success; participating together with Ingrid and my dear friend Linda Kauffman, our mentor, at Publix's Summer Triathlons series in Fort Lauderdale, Florida. Quite an accomplishment for all those of us who finished.

History repeats again, in having a very difficult situation which seriously affected my health. Starting September 2002 to February 2003, my personal status concerning my health issue seriously was back in peril while entangled in a complicated divorce that almost came close to sending me to the tomb. I implored the Lord through prayer for His prompt intervention, to bestow His blessing upon my soul, to overcome an unleashed, agonizing, living hell driven upon myself, none the least! In spite of injustice inflicted upon myself, I never succumbed to adversity; quite the contrary, I firmly was determined to hold my faith strong above all odds. Undoubtedly, I said it then and say it now, it probably had been the most devastating turn of events I have ever confronted since my adolescent years. Thus in the spirit of humility, prostrated on my knees, I implore my Lord forgiveness upon those individuals whose inhumane tactics succeeded in orchestrating such a horrendous episode.

On my 62ⁿᵈ birthday, November 15, 2004, after very deep soul searching, and consequently influenced by my brother, Roberto's astute brilliant advice, I reached an ultimate decision to officially announce my irrevocable retirement from the private sector after 41 years of service in the labor force. Apropos! Roberto convinced me that it was an act of greediness to wait until 65 years of age, just to collect more monies from a pension, rather than contemplate early retirement. Only God knew if I would die while waiting for those few years to pass, and consequently Uncle Sam would be the ultimate beneficiary of my pension.

It is worth mention that since my retirement back November 15, 2004, I still continued to be actively involved in voluntary work at West Boca Medical Center in Boca Raton, Florida. It really kept me occupied serving the public and hospital staff members who, day after day, I warmly used to welcome. That said, it was an unforgettable experience I shall carry for rest of my life.

Spring of year 2004, always will be remembered in my competitive sport records, by successfully reaching the finals of the senior open division at Patch Reef Park's Annual Tennis tournament " Splendor in the Grass." Little did I know that this would be the last time I would be participating in any tennis tournament event, ever indeed.

May of year 2005. Alas! With a high dose of faith and persistence, my dreams finally were realized when I was hired as a part time tennis aide position at Boca Raton Downtown Tennis Center, in the city of Boca Raton, Florida. Following almost 8 years of continuous frustration, and perennial denial from the City Hall Human Resources Department and City Park District officials, in spite of my tennis expertise credentials covering a quarter of a century, I was finally lucky to be hired thanks to a courtesy tip from my friend Peter Mascaro, whose unselfish prompt action was worth zillions, to say the least. God bless you eternally Don Peter.

April 15 year 2007, upon returning to New York, from Cali, Colombia. Roberto passed away at the age of 70 after suffering a massive stroke attack in the middle of the night. My consolation is that he succumbed to death according to his death wishes, "a quick eternal trip departure." Alleluia! He lived a good life, travelled to 4 Continents. He was my mentor and inspiration in my sports life, but overall, he was the instrumental savior on Earth during my life's most turbulent period, while fighting a terminal disease March year 1964. He really jumped all types of hurdles trying to find the best Hospital Institution possible, for me to have the best medical care during the first stage of my disease. That said, I shall be eternally grateful for your heroic actions brother.

March of year 2008 will be a date to reckon with in my life's annals. One of my most conscientious personal and spiritual decisions was reached by coming to my friend's rescue after she was sexually victimized. Against all odds, she was firmly determined, selecting to carry her pregnancy rather than contemplating an abortion. I instantly assumed my role as putative father to maximum dignity, which I profoundly did diligently and with satisfaction. On August 27, a healthy baby boy was born at Bethesda Memorial Hospital in Boynton Beach, Florida. Our offers of thanksgiving to the Lord, Amen! I always compare his fate similarly to Patriarch Moses, whose life was saved from an eminent assassination decree by the Egyptian Pharaoh, while left hidden at the Euphrates river bank shores.

At the beginning of November year 2008, following 3 ½ years of public relations serving patrons and visitors at the Boca Raton Tennis Center, my job maliciously was terminated in a horrendous maneuvering complot perpetrated by City Hall and

Park District officials. I was imputed of serious false charges; my reputation completely tarnished. And to make it worse, I absolutely was deprived from having legal professional representation; undoubtedly, a Bill of rights violation, impounding the law, to say the least. Since I was witness to a sexual harassment cover up inflicted upon a female coworker, officials were uncomfortably fearful that I was a man "who knew too much." History repeats once again, comparing my lower scale incident similarly to the assassination perpetrated against Emperor Julius Caesar year 1 BC by his Republic enemies and his best friend "Brutus;" mortally wounded Caesar kept screaming, "you too Brutus?" That is exactly how I felt screaming to my superiors, a pack of hyenas. That said, God forgive them. Unfortunately, I know who my traitors are. That is my fate.

May of year 2009, during a tennis mixed doubles social game, I sustained an injury in my groin, courtesy of Anabella Sibliss, as she executed a smash shot at the net. In the following year, February of 2010, I finally underwent the bistouries at North Broward General Hospital, Pompano Beach Florida. Later that night, post surgery, I underwent an indescribably agonizing experience; I really felt like dying, but not before hanging my dear Anabella from the tallest strong tree, indeed. Ha! Ha!

Enough is enough! That became my motto during year 2010, and I am referring to the ultimate decision I took to embark in a long overdue project, writing my memoirs which I previously had contemplated over 3 decades ago. I was encouraged by my dear friend and then coworker Joan Morsan, who I had once told the story of my miraculous survival 14 years earlier. I vividly remember very well when she advised me to write notes, keeping records pertaining to my miraculous recovery.

Summer of year 2011 after an 8 year span, I firmly reached the conclusion after deep soul searching that promises were made to be broken, and why not? When my previous marriage ended in a tragic battle royal, I solemnly promised never to get married again, but as time passed it proved me wrong. On July 26, precisely on my late mother's birthday anniversary, destiny had it, relinquishing my bachelor's statute. Thus once again I happily stepped over the threshold and became married to my beloved gorgeous Angel Maribell. The rest is just history, I simply went through another metamorphosis stage. God bless us, alleluia.

At last! October of year 2013, my adorable daughter Ingrid's 21 years of marriage came to a viciously disturbing end after 2 years of being subject to psychological and life threatening abuse, as proven by legal evidence. It turned out to be a very sad chapter in her life, and for all those whose existence she has touched. One very important mission I shall carry the rest of my life, Ingrid and Paul, both of you always will be remembered in my daily prayers until my life's last breath of air.

March 24 year 2014, a monumental day in my life, I celebrated half a century anniversary since I first was admitted into Elmhurst General Public Hospital with a preliminary unofficial diagnostic, a serious blood infection, a terminal disease, and 3 months to live, a hopeless condition indeed.

Last week of April, year 2014 another monumental commemoration marking a half century Anniversary once again, when I was admitted to Memorial Sloan Kettering James Ewing Center for Cancer and Allied Diseases, and enrolled in a voluntary Cancer Research program, an odyssey that lasted for over 11 plus years. I really consider myself blessed, a pilgrim of this World called upon to fulfill a missionary duty which the Lord has bestowed unto this humble servant, Amen.

Foremost, November 15 year 2014, I have reached 71 years of age, and at this stage of my existence I do arrive at the zenith conclusion that life is a dream, and my greatest personal satisfaction is unconditionally loving those whose life's I touch; family, relatives, friends, and enemies, as well. My beloved mother's words of wisdom, her advice inculcated unto me, paved the route which has been my own legacy, yes indeed.

Printed in the United States
by Baker & Taylor Publisher Services